the fall of man

JIMMY SWAGGART

JIMMY SWAGGART MINISTRIES
P.O. Box 262550 | Baton Rouge, Louisiana 70826-2550
www.jsm.org

ISBN 978-1-941403-34-1
09-144 | COPYRIGHT © 2017 Jimmy Swaggart Ministries®
17 18 19 20 21 22 23 24 25 26 / EBM / 10 9 8 7 6 5 4 3 2 1

TABLE OF CONTENTS

INTRODUCTION

the fall of man

INTRODUCTION

INTRODUCTION

AS IT REGARDS CREATION, whether of this material planet and universe or man—God's greatest creation—the only sensible account is given in the first two chapters of the book of Genesis in the Bible. Then, Chapter 3 of Genesis records the fall of man, which was a catastrophe of unprecedented proportions.

Regarding the account given in Genesis, Joseph Exell said:

The book of Genesis contains the history of the world's early progress, as presented in the lives of the most influential men of the times. It is therefore most important, certainly most interesting, and supremely reliable, as the outcome of a divine inspiration then for the first time given to man. The book has a doctrinal importance as well. It narrates the creation of man, with his temporal and moral surroundings. It teaches the divine origin of the soul; that life is a probation; that communion with God is a reality; that man is gifted with moral freedom; but he is subject to satanic influence, and that a violation of the law of God is the source of all human woe. Here we have the only reliable account of the introduction of sin into the world; the true philosophy of temptation, the true meaning of the redemptive purpose of God, the universal depravity of the early race, and we have exemplified the overruling providence of God in the history of all that is good.[1]

THE LORD JESUS CHRIST

If one wants to know what man was—as originally created by God—he only has to look at the Lord Jesus Christ. Our Lord was and is the perfect man, what God intended for man to be, and what man will ultimately be. An Adolf Hitler or a Joseph Stalin is not an account of what God has done, but an account of what Satan has done as it regards the fall of man. Jesus Christ says it all. As stated, if one wants to know what man was originally intended by God to be and the manner in which God created him, he need only look at Jesus Christ. As well, if one wants to know what God is like, and I speak, of course, of our heavenly Father, once again, he need only look at Jesus Christ.

Be Thou exalted, forever and ever,
God of eternity, the Ancient of Days!
Wondrous in majesty, so mighty in wisdom,
Perfect in holiness, and worthy of praise.

Be Thou exalted, O Son of the Highest
Gracious Redeemer, our Saviour and King!
One with the Father, coequal in glory,
Here at Your footstool our homage we bring.

Be Thou exalted, O Spirit eternal!
Dwell in our hearts, keep us holy within,
Feed us each day with Your heavenly manna,
Healer of wounded hearts, Your praises we sing.

the fall of man

CHAPTER 1

THE BEGINNING

THE BEGINNING

"IN THE BEGINNING GOD created the heaven and the earth" (Gen. 1:1).

The phrase, *"In the beginning,"* speaks of a time in eternity past when God began the creation of the heavens and the earth. Williams says, "Beginning is the subject of this book; it teaches that God is the beginner of the visible and invisible universe, as He is the beginner of salvation in the soul of the sinner."[1]

We aren't told here when this beginning took place, only that it happened sometime in eternity past.

God has always existed, which means there never was a time when He didn't exist. As such, and knowing that He is a creator, which is an essential part of His being (Jn. 5:17), we are made to wonder what existed before the heavens and the earth; however, any idea is speculation at best, and when it comes to God, it's best not to speculate.

GOD

The theory of evolution puts forth all types of speculation as it regards the creation of man along with the heavens and the earth.

However, irrespective of the proposals they make, they have absolutely no idea of the first cause. Every hypothesis they put forth is always based on existing materials of some kind; consequently, not having a proper foundation, their hypotheses are always wrong.

The phrase, *"In the beginning God,"* gives the first cause. That first cause is God.

God in the Hebrew is *Elohim.* Its root meaning is "strength and power." *Elohim* is a uniplural noun, which shows the plurality of persons in the Godhead. Consequently, from the very beginning, we see the doctrine of three divine persons in the unity of the Godhead. There is one God but manifest in three persons—God the Father, God the Son, and God the Holy Spirit.

To help us understand the Trinity and creation a little better, perhaps the following may shed some light: God the Father is the divine owner; God the Son is the divine architect; and God the Holy Spirit is the divine builder. And yet, whatever is said of each member of the Trinity can be said of all the members.

TRINITY

The word *Trinity* is not found in the Bible. It was used, it is said, by Tertullian, in the last decade of the second century, but it did not really find a place formally in the theology of the church until the fourth century. It is, however, the distinctive and all-comprehensive doctrine of the Christian faith.

It makes three affirmations: That there is but one God; that the Father, the Son, and the Spirit are each God; and that the Father, the Son, and the Spirit are each a distinct person. In this form, it has become the faith of the church.

With the revelation of the Lord Jesus Christ, the Trinity comes much more into view.

For instance, when the angel Gabriel appeared to Mary, He said that the Holy Spirit would come upon her. He then added that the power of the Most High would overshadow her and that the child born of her would be called *"the Son of God"* (Lk. 1:35). In this, we see the Trinity—the Father and the Spirit functioning in the incarnation of the Son.

At the baptism of Christ in the Jordan River, three persons of the Godhead can be distinguished there. The Son is the one being baptized; the Father is speaking from heaven in recognition of His Son; and the Spirit is descending as a dove upon Jesus (Jn. 1:32–33).

TRINITARIAN

The teaching of Jesus is Trinitarian throughout. He spoke of the Father who sent Him, of Himself as the one who reveals the Father, and the Spirit as the one by whom He and the Father work. In fact, the interrelations between Father, Son, and Spirit are emphasized throughout (Jn. 14:7, 9–10). He declared with emphasis: *"I will pray the Father, and He shall give you another Comforter* (Advocate), *that He may abide with you forever; even the Spirit of truth"* (Jn. 14:16–26). There is thus a distinction and also an identity made between the persons of the Godhead. The Father, who is God, sent the Son, and the Son, who is God, sent the Spirit, who is Himself God.

In the commission given by Christ before His ascension, instructing His disciples to go into the whole world with His message, He made specific reference to baptism as *"in the name of the Father, and of the Son, and of the Holy Spirit."* It is significant that the name is one, but within the bounds of the one name, there are three distinct persons. In fact, the Trinity as triunity could not be more clearly expressed (Mat. 28:19).

Early Christians knew themselves to be reconciled to God the Father, that the reconciliation was secured for them by the atoning work of the Son, and that it was mediated to them as an experience by the Holy Spirit. Thus, the Trinity was to them a fact before it became a doctrine.

CREATION

The phrase, *"Created the heaven and the earth,"* proclaims such being done sometime in eternity past. Concerning Verse 1 in Genesis, Matthew Henry said, "The first verse of the Bible gives a surer and better, a more satisfying and useful knowledge of the origin of the universe, than all the volumes of the philosophers." He then went on to say, "The lively faith of humble Christians understands this matter better than the elevated fancy of the most learned."[2]

Creation, in its strict sense, carries the meaning of producing something out of nothing. Naturally, that is impossible as it regards man, but it is not impossible with God. Jesus said, *"With God all things are possible"* (Mat. 19:26). In fact, God spoke the creation into existence (Heb. 11:3), which we shall see in the following verses. Why is it so hard for man to believe that?

As stated, Moses did not bother to explain the fact that there is a God. The idea is that creation demands a creator. Common sense tells us that, but common sense seems to be in short supply.

WITHOUT FORM AND VOID

"And the earth was without form, and void; and darkness was upon the face of the deep. And the Spirit of God moved upon the face of the waters" (Gen. 1:2).

God did not originally create the earth without form and void. It became that way after a cataclysmic happening. This cataclysmic happening was the revolt of Lucifer against God, which took place in the dateless past. As a result, darkness was upon the face of the deep.

The moving of the Holy Spirit upon the face of the waters— done in order to bring the earth back to a habitable state—was the beginning of life.

The phrase, *"And the earth was without form, and void,"* points to a stupendous convulsion that affected the earth after it was created by God.

"Without form, and void," in the Hebrew is literally *tohu* and *bohu,* which signify "wasteness and emptiness." God did not create the earth in this fashion. It became that way at a point in time. Many scholars believe that Lucifer ruled the earth after it

was originally created, and did so in righteousness for an undetermined period of time. As well, during that time, he ruled it in
righteousness and holiness under God. It also seems there was
a race of created beings over whom he ruled. Whenever Lucifer
led his rebellion against God, one-third of the angels, plus this
race of beings, threw in their lot with him. Many think, and it
is probably correct, that these particular beings, whatever they
might have been, are the demon spirits that presently help Satan.

Some have claimed that demon spirits are fallen angels;
however, angels have spirit-bodies, whereas demon spirits have
no body whatsoever and, in fact, seek a body to inhabit, whether
animal or human.

I think it should be obvious that whatever degree
this revolution of Lucifer was, its destructive power was
beyond comprehension.

THE MYSTERY OF GOD

Knowing that God is omnipotent (all-powerful), omniscient
(all-knowing), and omnipresent (everywhere), and that Lucifer
was and is a mere creature, we may wonder why the Lord has
allowed the Evil One to continue this long. The Scripture refers
to this as the *"mystery of God"* (Rev. 10:7). Why the Lord has
allowed this, we are not told; however, we do know that God
does all things well, and everything He does is done for a purpose and reason and is always the right thing to do.

Irrespective of what has happened in the past, and even
how it has affected man, this one thing we do know: God has

effected redemption for mankind through the giving of His Son, the Lord Jesus Christ, who, by His death at the Cross, brought about four great judicial results.

They are:

1. Calvary effected the acknowledgment in the person of Christ, the act of the due judgment that the sin-principle required. In other words, judgment was poured out on Christ instead of on mankind, at least for those who will believe (Jn. 3:16).

2. Calvary made it possible for corrupted self, of which Satan is the personal author and representative, to be placed in Christ. As someone has well said, Jesus died on the Cross in order to save man from self as well as from sin (Gal. 2:20–21).

3. Calvary destroyed the organic connection that Satan had brought about between sin and death. While the wages of sin continue to be death, Calvary made it possible for that connection to be assuaged by the blood of Christ (I Jn. 1:7). In other words, spiritual death as a result of sin, of which all men are guilty, no longer claims its victims, at least as it regards those who have accepted Christ.

4. Calvary made possible the adjudgment of all men to the Redeemer as His personal possession, that is, those who will believe (I Cor. 6:20).

THAT WHICH JESUS DID AT THE CROSS

Thus, by this fourfold achievement that was carried out at Calvary, the judicial expression of Christ's work on the Cross extended to the deepest realities of the moral universe. In effect, it anticipated every essential moral issue that the soul would need to fear in view of its own misgivings concerning destiny.

The punishment difficulty with respect to past sin was potentially met. Satan, man's archenemy, was potentially destroyed, the causation between sin and death was potentially broken, and the claim of Christ to the possession of all men was potentially set up.

Thus, in dealing with the ultimate spiritual realities of the universe, Christ's Cross was, in effect, the anticipation of the final judgment of all mankind.

In fact, the early triumphs of Christianity were won upon the basis of the conception of Christ's death, as such, a judicial transaction. Actually, this was the heart of Paul's message (Rom. 6:3–14; 8:1–11; I Cor. 1:17–18, 21, 23; 2:2, 5; Col. 2:10-15).

The mystery of God will be finished at the second coming when Satan will be locked away in the bottomless pit (Rev. 20:1–3).

However, the ground was laid for his total defeat by what Christ did at the Cross, without which, the Evil One would have triumphed.

Christ alone could take the book from the hand of God the Father because He alone was worthy, and He was worthy because of what He did at the Cross (Rev. 5:8–9).

DARKNESS

The phrase, *"And darkness was upon the face of the deep,"* represents the end result of satanic influence, which is the opposite of light. The light represents God.

There is what is referred to as the "gap theory," which belongs between Verse 1 and Verse 2. As previously stated, this is the particular time that Lucifer rebelled against God. Actually, the word *deep* is from a root signifying "to disturb."

The ruin pictured in this verse reveals the sinner prior to regeneration. The remainder of the chapter describes the renewing power of the Spirit of God introducing light, life, and beauty from out of this ruin. The created energy of the Holy Spirit operates presently in a similar manner in the ruined nature of man. Believers become new creations (II Cor. 5:17) and are created unto good works (Eph. 2:10).

It took the Cross to dispel this darkness because the darkness was more than mere surface. It went all the way to the disturbed deep. In other words, it was total darkness.

The Cross opened up the way to God and made it possible for light to once again shine, of which this verse is a type.

THE SPIRIT OF GOD

The phrase, *"And the Spirit of God moved upon the face of the waters,"* presents the beginning of life, i.e., re-creation. Because it is so important, please allow me to say it again: The moving of the Holy Spirit is the beginning of life.

We will find that every act of the Godhead carried out on this earth is done through the person, agency, work, power, ministry, and office of the Holy Spirit. The only exception to that would be the ministry of Christ in this world in His first advent, but even then, the Holy Spirit functioned in every single capacity of His conception, birth, life, ministry, death, and resurrection (Lk. 4:18–19).

This corresponds with the statement we have previously made, to use the vernacular, God the Father is the owner, God the Son is the architect, and God the Holy Spirit is the builder. But yet, one could use any of these designations for any one of the Trinity, and it would be correct.

Psalm 33:6 tells us that God made the world by His Spirit, and one might quickly say that by the same mighty worker, the new creation is effected in the soul.

The Holy Spirit works exclusively within the parameters of the finished work of Christ.

There is every evidence that in the mind of God, even before this particular time, God through foreknowledge knew that He would create man and that man would fall.

It was determined in the mind of the Godhead that man would be redeemed by God becoming man in order to go to the Cross, where the price would be paid for man's redemption.

Peter said: *"Forasmuch as you know that you were not redeemed with corruptible things, as silver and gold ... But with the precious blood of Christ, as of a lamb without blemish and without spot: Who verily was foreordained before the foundation of the world, but was manifest in these last times for you"* (I Pet. 1:18–20).

THE HOLY SPIRIT

From this moment of re-creation, the Holy Spirit has been in the world. He superintended the giving of the word of a limited reconciliation to the first family immediately after the fall. This is carried out in Genesis, Chapter 4, and is summed up in the sacrifices, which epitomized the coming Christ.

Up unto the time of the Cross, which was about 4,000 years from the time of the fall, the Holy Spirit was limited in what He could do because the terrible sin debt hung over the heads of all of humanity.

The blood of bulls and goats could not take away sin, so the debt remained (Heb. 10:4). As a result, when the saints of God died who lived before the Cross, Satan could still claim them as his captives, which he definitely did; consequently, their souls and spirits went down into paradise. Because the sin debt was still there, they could not be taken to heaven when they died (Lk. 16:20–31).

However, when Jesus died on the Cross and, thereby, atoned for all sin, which removed the sin debt, He went down into paradise, which was in the heart of the earth.

Concerning that visit, Paul said: *"Wherefore He said, When He ascended up on high, He led captivity captive, and gave gifts unto men. (Now that He ascended, what is it but that He also descended first into the lower parts of the earth?"* (Eph. 4:8–9).

LEADING CAPTIVITY CAPTIVE

The term *"He led captivity captive,"* is strange, but it means the following: As stated, every person in paradise, which included all the patriarchs and prophets of old, were actually held captive there by Satan. He could not put them over into the burning side of the pit, but, still, they were his captives. However, when Jesus paid the price on the Cross, He went down into paradise and took those who were captives of Satan and made them His captives. He did this because now the sin debt was paid by what He did at the Cross. In other words, Satan had no more claim on them, and neither does he have claim on any believer in the world today.

Now, when believers die, due to what Jesus did at the Cross, their souls and spirits automatically go to heaven to be with the Lord (Phil. 1:23).

Concerning how the Holy Spirit works within our hearts and lives as it regards our sanctification, Paul said, *"For the law* (a law devised by the Godhead) *of the Spirit of life* (Holy Spirit) *in Christ Jesus* (this law is based on what Jesus did at the Cross) *has made me free from the law of sin and death"* (Rom. 8:2).

To sum up, every single thing the Holy Spirit has done in this world, is doing, and shall do is based entirely on the Cross of Christ. The Cross is what makes everything possible (I Cor. 1:17).

THE WORD OF GOD

"And God said, Let there be light: and there was light" (Gen. 1:3).

The phrase, *"And God said,"* presents the manner in which creation, or re-creation, was carried out. Some 10 times this phrase is used in this exact manner, with the exception of the last time, where it says, *"And the LORD God said"* (Gen. 2:18).

By the use of the term, *"And God said,"* we are given very little information. Probably, the phrase, then, is metaphorical and actually means that God enacted for the universe a law.

However, from these three words, we do learn some things. First of all, we learn from this that God makes no preparation, employs no means, and needs no secondary agency. He speaks, and it is done. His Word alone contains all things necessary for the fulfillment of His will. By speaking, God gives to nature a universal and enduring law.

As well, His commands are not temporary but eternal; and whatever secondary causes were called into existence when God, by a word, created light, those same causes produce it now and will produce it until God recalls His word. We have then, here, nature's first universal law.

LIGHT

The phrase, *"Let there be light: and there was light,"* presents the first universal law.

Are we to understand that this light now brought into being by God was independent of the sun, the moon, etc.? Calvin and Augustine said that it was; however, I think not! God certainly could have spoken light into existence without the sun, etc.

Nevertheless, I think the light came from the sun, and what we see in Verses 14 through 18 speaks of the regulation of the sun, moon, and stars.

Light travels at the speed of 186,000 miles a second. Incidentally, we are told that the universe is expanding at that particular rate, which means that the Word of God saying, *"Let there be light,"* is still at work.

THE LIGHT WAS GOOD

"And God saw the light, that it was good: and God divided the light from the darkness" (Gen. 1:4).

The phrase, *"And God saw the light, that it was good,"* refers to the fact that what it was designed to do, it would do.

It was designed not merely for illumination, although that certainly is one of its great purposes, but, as well, plants have to have light to survive and grow. So, there is a life-giving property of sorts in this light made by God.

LIGHT AND DARKNESS

The phrase, *"And God divided the light from the darkness,"* does not imply that darkness has a separate and independent existence, but that there were now periods of light and darkness.

Taking this particular statement of the dividing of light from darkness into the spiritual sense, we know that light and darkness can never be joined together. As the Scripture says: *"And have no fellowship with the unfruitful works of darkness"* (Eph. 5:11).

In heaven, there is nothing but perpetual light, while in hell, there is perpetual darkness (Mat. 8:12; Rev. 21:23–25).

This which we are studying is the first day of the week. Likewise, Christ rose from the dead on the first day of the week. It carries the aura of a new beginning.

DAY

"And God called the light day, and the darkness He called night. And the evening and the morning were the first day" (Gen. 1:5).

By using the phraseology, *"The evening and the morning were the first day,"* we know these were literal 24-hour days.

The phrase, *"And God called the light day,"* is not meant to be a time measure, but rather a character description. But yet, as we shall see, at this particular time, the word *day* is part of a 24-hour period.

NIGHT

The phrase, *"And the darkness He called night,"* has to do with the revolution of the earth. In the manner in which God made man, the work and rest cycle is figured into this 24-hour revolution of the earth.

THE FIRST DAY

Some claim that these were not 24-hour days, but rather undetermined periods of time, but the phrasing, *"The evening and the morning were the first day,"* as stated, limits these days to a 24-hour time period. The word *day* can be used to designate any period of time and is often used that way. However, the attaching of the words *evening* and *morning* seem to nail it down that in this instance, God is speaking of a literal 24-hour time period.

The idea that the word *day,* as it is used in this chapter, represents some indefinite time period, possibly even thousands of years, is mostly because men doubt the ability of God to bring all of this about in such a short period of time. However long God took to bring the earth back to a habitable state is really of no consequence, but I think enough scriptural evidence is given to nail down the 24-hour time frame. While it's certainly not proper to overstate the case, it's not proper either to understate it. Understating the case always limits God, while it is virtually impossible to overstate the case as it regards God. He is able to do all things.

FIRMAMENT

"And God said, Let there be a firmament in the midst of the waters, and let it divide the waters from the waters" (Gen. 1:6).

Firmament in the Hebrew means "expansion." God divided the waters, making the oceans and the seas on one side, or as one might say, on the bottom, and their clouds, with the ability to give rain, on the top, with a clear space between. Had not the waters been divided by the atmosphere, human life could not exist.

The phrase, *"And God said, Let there be a firmament in the midst of the waters,"* refers to an expanse between the waters, so to speak, called "the atmosphere."

While most probably have never given it much thought, the atmosphere is necessary for the transmission of sound. If there were no atmosphere, the bell could ring, but it could not be heard. The music could play, but it could not be heard. The voices could lift up on high as they sing the anthems of glory, but there would be no sound. So, we see that all of this was actually made for man.

DIVIDE THE WATERS

The phrase, *"And let it divide the waters from the waters,"* refers to the fact that before this was done, not only was there water all over the earth, but, as well, it seems that water also filled the expanse that we refer to as the atmosphere. The Lord divided these waters and separated the clouds, with some of them filled with water, i.e., rain, from the waters that covered part of the surface of the earth.

AND GOD MADE

"And God made the firmament, and divided the waters which were under the firmament from the waters which were above the firmament: and it was so" (Gen. 1:7).

The waters *"under the firmament"* pertain to the oceans, seas, rivers, etc. The waters *"above the firmament"* pertain to the water that's in the clouds, which comes down as rain upon the earth.

The phrase, *"And God made the firmament,"* refers to the wide-open expanse above earth's surface, reaching up to the clouds and beyond, with that marvelous mixture of gases that form atmospheric air, which are necessary for man's existence and activity.

WATERS UNDER AND OVER THE FIRMAMENT

The phrase, *"And divided the waters which were under the firmament from the waters which were above the firmament: and it was so,"* is not contrary to, but in accordance with, science.

The creation that God has devised presents the laws by which rain is formed and the earth watered. This is constantly referred to in the Bible as the chief natural proof of God's wisdom and goodness (Acts 14:17).

Six times the phrase, *"And it was so,"* is used. It speaks of the resistless energy of the divine Word. As creation functions accordingly, we should, as well, function, always eager to do the will of God, so much so, in fact, that His Word becomes our command.

HEAVEN

"And God called the firmament heaven. And the evening and the morning were the second day" (Gen. 1:8).

"Heaven," as referred to here, pertains to the atmosphere around the earth.

God adjusted the firmament on the second day of re-creation.

The work of the second day is not mentioned as being good because the work of day three had to be carried out before this part was complete.

The phrase, *"And God called the firmament heaven,"* is not the same meaning regarding heaven as in Verse 1.

In Verse 1, *"the heaven"* refers to the entirety of the universe. *"Heaven"* in Verse 8 refers to the atmosphere around the earth, which goes up about 45 miles from the surface before it begins to lose its gravitational pull.

The phrase, *"And the evening and the morning were the second day,"* as well, speaks of a 24-hour time frame.

OCEANS AND SEAS

"And God said, Let the waters under the heaven be gathered together unto one place, and let the dry land appear: and it was so" (Gen. 1:9).

Water had heretofore covered the face of the earth but was now gathered into oceans and seas.

The dry land, i.e., continents, now appeared. At the word of God, there evidently were mighty convulsions on the earth, which pulled the land mass up and created a lower mass for the oceans.

The phrase, *"And God said, Let the waters under the heaven be gathered together unto one place,"* evidently means that before this, water covered the entirety of the surface of the earth. God would speak, and the earth would go into convulsions, which made the mountains and the landmass. This, of necessity, made the lower mass where the great oceans and seas were contained.

While the oceans cover a great part of this world, it is evidently only just sufficient to supply the rain necessary for vegetation. Were it less, either the laws of evaporation must be altered, with painful and injurious effects, or much of the earth's surface would be barren.

In the new earth to come, the Scripture says, *"There was no more sea"* (Rev. 21:1). So, at that time, the evaporation process regarding rain, etc., will have to be changed, which it, no doubt, will, along with many other things also. In fact, concerning this very thing, the Lord said, *"Behold, I make all things new"* (Rev. 21:5).

CONTINENTS

The phrase, *"And let the dry land appear: and it was so,"* refers to the continents being formed, which, as stated, necessitated great convulsions on the earth in many and varied forms.

The psalmist said concerning God:

Who laid the foundations of the earth, that it should not be removed forever. You cover it with the deep as with a garment: the waters stood above the mountains. At Your rebuke they fled; at the voice of Your thunder they hasted away. They go up by the mountains; they go down by the valleys unto the place which You have founded for them. You have set a bound that they may not pass over; that they turn not again to cover the earth (Ps. 104:5–9).

The Holy Spirit through the psalmist is referring to this particular work of day three.

EARTH AND SEAS

"And God called the dry land earth; and the gathering together of the waters called He seas: and God saw that it was good" (Gen. 1:10).

The phrase, *"And God called the dry land earth,"* refers to the Supreme Being naming what He had created.

The phrase, *"And the gathering together of the waters called He seas,"* pertains to God naming this creation, as well, and, incidentally, names that have survived from then until now.

In the Hebrew, earth is *shamayim* and seas is *yamim.*

IT IS GOOD

"God saw that it was good," refers to the finished product, at least at this stage, as being sealed by the divine approval.

GRASS

"And God said, Let the earth bring forth grass, the herb yielding seed, and the fruit tree yielding fruit after his kind, whose seed is in itself, upon the earth: and it was so" (Gen. 1:11).

Three types of vegetation are spoken into existence:

1. Grass is brought forth as a carpet.

2. *"The herb"* speaks of vegetables.

3. Various different kinds of fruit trees come forth.

"After his kind" indicates that the different species of plants are already fixed.

"And God said, Let the earth bring forth grass," pertains to the first sprouts of the earth—tender herbs, in which the seed is so small it's not noticed. It serves as a carpet for the earth, and at the same time, food for certain animals (Ps. 23:2).

The first creative act of God was the calling of matter into existence, which, by the operation of mechanical and chemical laws imposed upon it by the Creator, was arranged and digested into a cosmos, that is, an orderly and harmonious whole.

These laws are now and ever in perpetual activity, but no secondary or derived agency can either add one atom to the world-mass or diminish aught from it.

The second creative act is the introduction of light, then vegetable, then animal; and for this, nothing less than an almighty power would suffice.

HERBS

"The herb yielding seed," refers to vegetables eaten by man, etc. It is a higher form of plant life than grass.

Nothing here is mentioned about the different types of trees and certain other types of plant life, with the intent seemingly emphasizing that which can be used as food, whether for animals or humans.

However, one may conclude that the other types of trees, etc., were created at this time as well.

THE FRUIT TREE

"And the fruit tree yielding fruit after his kind, whose seed is in itself, upon the earth: and it was so," presents yet a more advanced creation, one might say.

The Pulpit Commentary says: "This division is simple and natural. It proceeds from two concurrent marks, the structure and the seed. In the first the green blade is prominent; in the second, the stalk; in the third, the woody texture; in the first (grass) the seed is not conspicuous; in the second it is conspicuous; in the third it is enclosed in a fruit which is conspicuous."[3]

By the use of the phrase, *"After his kind,"* it pertains to both vegetables and fruit, indicating that the different species of plants were already fixed.

Thus, the modern dogma of the origin of species by development would be declared to be unbiblical as it has not yet been proven to be scientific and, in fact, will never be proven in that capacity simply because a slow development is not actually what happened.

It is God's word that makes the earth fruitful. Propagation of fruit, as well as the first being of it, is by God's word; He makes the seed and enables it to multiply.

YIELDING SEED AFTER HIS KIND

"And the earth brought forth grass, and herb yielding seed after his kind, and the tree yielding fruit, whose seed was in itself, after

his kind: and God saw that it was good. And the evening and the morning were the third day" (Gen. 1:12-13).

At the word of God, the earth brought forth that which God commanded.

"After his kind," regards the different species that God ordained.

God pronounced it *"good."*

The bringing forth of this plant life, which is food for animals and humans, was the work of the third day, a 24-hour period.

AFTER HIS KIND

"And the earth brought forth grass, and herb yielding seed after his kind, and the tree yielding fruit, whose seed was in itself, after his kind," proclaims the bringing forth of this foodstuff by the word of God because the atmosphere had been created for its development, which was brought forth on days one and two.

All of this tells us that the first creation of plant life did not come from seed, but it came into being through the power of the word.

Continuing with the power of the word, the seed now has power to grow and reproduce. It is by special divine power that a kernel, put into soil, comes up in its appointed time and bears fruit according to its kind.

This shows that the creation, according to which every plant is produced after its kind in its proper order, is not a matter of chance but a preeminent work of divine providence.

IT WAS GOOD

"And God saw that it was good," proclaims not only the fact of creation but, as well, the order of creation.

Some have asked the question of why God would have developed plant life before He brought into being the stars of the heavens, etc.

As we shall see, the heavens, including the stars, along with the sun and the moon, had already been created. This was done in the beginning. On the fourth day, God would regulate them.

God's attention to the earth was because the earth was now being re-created for man. He would actually prepare all things for man, even before man was created.

Incidentally, the third day presents the first creation of life, i.e., the plants, etc.

LIGHTS

"And God said, Let there be lights in the firmament of the heaven to divide the day from the night; and let them be for signs, and for seasons, and for days, and years" (Gen. 1:14).

As we have stated, God was not creating here the sun, moon, and stars, with that having already been done in the beginning.

He was here regulating them as to their functions.

They would be for signs, seasons, days, and years.

"And God said, Let there be lights in the firmament of the heaven to divide the day from the night," pertains to the expanse of the heavens of outer space. In fact, these lights, i.e., sun, moon, and

stars, had already been created. This was done in the beginning, whenever that was in the dateless past. The giving forth of these lights doesn't change. It's the rotation of the earth that divides the day from the night, but that rotation has to do with the gravitational pull of the planetary bodies.

Some have asked, "What is the difference between the 'light' of Verse 3 and of Verse 14?" I don't think there is any difference. I think they are one and the same.

The planetary bodies, and especially the sun, are brought back to a serviceable state in Verse 3 and are regulated in Verse 14.

SEASONS

The phrase, *"And let them be for signs, and for seasons, and for days, and years,"* refers, in essence, to time. By the moon's four quarters, which last each a little more than seven days, the weeks and the months are measured for us. The sun, by its apparent path in the sky, measures our seasons and our years, while by its daily rotation through the heavens, it measures the days and the hours. This it does so correctly, never varying, that the astronauts can depend on it as they make their reentry to earth from space. Otherwise, they would invite certain death.

It has been well said that the progress of a people in civilization may be estimated by their regard for time—their care in measuring and valuing it. Our time is a loan. It is God's gift to us. We must use it as faithful stewards, and to be sure, we shall have to give an account of its use. O Lord, *"So teach us to number our days, that we may apply our hearts unto wisdom"* (Ps. 90:12).

David said, *"Evening, and morning, and at noon, will I pray, and cry aloud: and He shall hear my voice"* (Ps. 55:17).

Concerning this great work of creation, David also said, *"When I consider Your heavens, the work of Your fingers, the moon and the stars, which You have ordained; what is man, that You are mindful of him? and the son of man, that You visit him?"* (Ps. 8:3-4).

TO GIVE LIGHT UPON THE EARTH

"And let them be for lights in the firmament of the heaven to give light upon the earth: and it was so" (Gen. 1:15).

This proclaims the fact that God said it, and His glorious word contained such power that these planetary bodies will ever carry out their prescribed function.

Though the sun and the planets are so far distant from us, yet this does not interrupt their light and influence. The spiritual lesson we must derive from that is distance cannot hinder us from receiving the benefit of God's care. Though God's influence is in heaven, His eye beholds the children of men. So, we aren't to allow distance, either in place or condition, to hinder our desires for the good of others.

CREATED AND MADE

"And God made two great lights; the greater light to rule the day, and the lesser light to rule the night: He made the stars also" (Gen. 1:16).

This alludes to the sun and the moon. In fact, the moon has no light within itself. It is a reflection of the sun, hence, much lesser, exactly as the Scripture says.

Modern man scoffs at the idea that God, merely by His word, could make the sun, plus all the planetary bodies, and even the universe. He scoffs, as well, at God's creation of man and, actually, the entirety of all things as they were created by God. In essence, he denies that there is a God!

The words *created* and *made* should be distinguished when they are read. The difficulties that science—imperfect and limited—finds here have been satisfactorily discussed by able commentators, and their arguments need not be repeated, except to draw attention to these important and distinctive words—*created* and *made.*

For example, the Lord *created* the sun, moon, and stars at some unknown period of time in the beginning. Afterward, when preparing the earth for man, He *made,* i.e., pointed them in relation to the earth (regulated them) as light-holders, as measurers of time, and as vehicles of revelation (Ps. 19).

GOD

"And God set them in the firmament of the heaven to give light upon the earth, and to rule over the day and over the night, and to divide the light from the darkness: and God saw that it was good. And the evening and the morning were the fourth day" (Gen. 1:17-19).

The life of man is governed here largely by the order of the material universe, but as he becomes a true child of God, he rises to a dominion over the sun, moon, and stars. In fact, the con-sciousness of fellowship with God is a sense of moral superiority to material things. Man is earthly first and then heavenly. Human nature is developed under the rule of sun, moon, and stars, but is warped and twisted because of sin. In the world to come, where there shall be no more night, the consciousness of man will then be far more spiritual than material, not unwitting of the material, but ruling it with spiritual freedom and power (Rev., Chpt. 22).

ANIMATE LIFE

"And God said, Let the waters bring forth abundantly the moving creature that has life, and fowl that may fly above the earth in the open firmament of heaven" (Gen. 1:20).

Verse 20 proclaims the creation of fish and birds. The Pulpit Commentary says, "Here the creatures of the sea are distin-guished from all previous creations, and in particular from vegetation, as being possessed of a vital principle; this does not, of course, contradict the well-known truth that plants are living organisms; only that the life principle of the animal kingdom is different from that of the vegetable kingdom."[4]

The way Verse 20 is translated leaves the impression that the fish and the fowl were made from the waters; however, Genesis 2:19 refutes that. The idea is, the *"waters"* (seas, rivers, lakes, oceans) swarmed with every kind of fish. Exactly how God created the fish, for instance, we aren't told. It was probably done by divine command. As it regards the *"fowl of the air,"* Genesis 2:19 says that the Lord formed these *"out of the ground."*

AFTER HIS KIND

"And God created great whales, and every living creature that moves, which the waters brought forth abundantly, after their kind, and every winged fowl after his kind: and God saw that it was good" (Gen. 1:21).

By the use of the phrases, *"After their kind"* and *"after his kind,"* this verse emphasizes the different species that are created.

Some 10 times in Chapter 1 of Genesis, the phrase, *"After his kind,"* or similar, is used. This completely shoots down the theory of evolution. Science has never been able to cross that barrier and, in fact, will never be able. In other words, there is no such thing as an animal that is half fish and half land animal. As well, there is no such thing as a fish that is half whale and half shark. The barrier regarding the different kinds remains and ever shall remain.

The same can be said for man. There is no such thing as a creature that is half man and half animal. To be sure, if evolution were a true science, there would be some evidence of such in the world. False science answers that by claiming that the evolutionary process takes many millions or even billions of years; however, even if that were true, which it's not, there would still be some creatures in the world that are part animal and part man. In fact, there would be mutations of every kind.

MUTATIONS

If the rabbit did actually evolve from the frog, or whatever, there would be scores of creatures at different stages. However, that doesn't exist and, in fact, has never existed because the iron barrier of *"after his kind,"* as originally created by God, cannot be changed. While man can produce a mule by the crossbreeding of a horse and a donkey, the mule is then sterile and cannot reproduce itself.

Actually, the evolutionary process fails in every capacity. Plants, for instance, do not get better and better, but rather tend to degenerate if left on their own, which is the opposite of the so-called evolutionary process.

To make plants better or fruit trees bear more luscious fruit, man has to work with these plants or trees in order to bring out their best.

It is the same with horses. If the breed is left unattended, it will degenerate. So, man has to work with horses in the realm of breeding to perfect thoroughbreds, etc.

There are at least two processes that debunk evolution:

1. The first is the iron barrier of the species, which cannot be crossed.

2. The second problem is degeneration, even as we have already addressed.

EVOLUTION

Can a person be a Christian and also believe in evolution? No, he cannot. To believe in evolution is to disbelieve the Bible, and to disbelieve the Bible is to disbelieve God.

Some so-called Christians attempt to cover this by claiming that they believe in creation, and that God is the one who has created all things, but that He did it by evolution. Once again, this flies in the face of the Word of God.

Not only is evolution unbiblical, but at the same time, it is unscientific. I read just the other day of the death of a particular man in England, who exposed the Piltdown hoax. This was a skeleton found in a certain part of England, which was supposed to prove the evolutionary process. He found that the skeleton had been doctored with plaster of Paris, or whatever, to make it seem to be something it wasn't. He exposed the fraud, which meant that many schoolbooks had to be rewritten.

If the evolutionary conception is true, it naturally follows that the biblical account cannot be accepted in its literal interpretation. One of these accounts pictures the different species and general types as coming into existence gradually out of preexisting ones, whereas the other represents them as created by a divine fiat.

THE BIBLE AND EVOLUTION
CANNOT BE HARMONIZED

All efforts to harmonize Genesis with evolution lead at best to the negative conclusion that these two are so far different in their purpose and scope as not to involve radical contradiction. A positive agreement between them simply cannot be claimed.

The general theories of evolution are not proving true in either the biological or geological field. This fact is so true that one scientific observer has aptly remarked that the present vogue of these theories in the popular and pseudo-scientific mind may be likened to the continued, though dwindling, activities of a central commercial trust, whose supporting subsidiary companies had all gone into bankruptcy. Furthermore, it is highly significant that many, who at first were fascinated by the generalizations of evolution, turned from it after further examination of its proffered evidences and more mature consideration of its claims.

The truth is, evolution is not a fact of science but a dogma of philosophy. Both its history and its essential nature prove that it belongs primarily to the realm of subjective speculation and not to the field of objective fact.

UNCHRISTIAN

It is significant that the idea of evolution originated in heathen and pagan minds and was not a native product of the Christian intellect, which means that it's not biblical.

The general run of modern definitions of evolution is also not only completely independent of any thought of a living God but, for the most part, is either directly antagonistic to that thought or irreconcilable with it. In fact, the standard definitions of evolution, which are given by real evolutionists, are, therefore, consistently and completely in line with anti-God theories.

Actually, as it regards evolution, that is, if one takes it to its final conclusion, there is no God and no need for God. In fact, all definitions of evolution, of necessity, have to substitute blind force and mere chance for the creative power of a living God. Those who try to reconcile these theories with the Christian system of truth assert that such is not the case, yet the definitions given—and many others that might be given—prove that God is, of necessity, ruled out in favor of chance. Evolution must be seen to be diametrically opposed to the Christian system of thought at all essential points.

OPPOSED TO REAL CHRISTIANITY

Some claim that an all-powerful God could have made the world and created man and woman by evolutionary process if He had so desired and willed. However, the Bible revelation tells us that He did not so make the world, man, and woman, and that we may stand upon that revelation with full assurance. In the words of Professor Mullins, Professor Machen, and Dr. Conrad, evolution leads to a type of religion that is radically different from Christianity and, as well, diametrically opposed to Bible Christianity.

A final and conclusive consideration in this whole problem of alleged evolution is that there is evidence on all sides, going to prove that the whole world and all that is in it is running down, degenerating, and moving toward some climax of judgment and re-creation, even as the Bible says, instead of ever evolving upward into higher and better forms.

CHEMISTRY

It is most significant that in the science of chemistry, through which we come closest to the deeper facts and forces of both inanimate matter and life, there is no evidence of any resident *urge* upward. Not only is it true that the laws of chemical affinity seem to be static and unchangeable as to their operations, but it is now known that there is a disintegrating tendency downward instead of upward that seems characteristic of all matter. In other words, there is a degeneration, even as previously stated.

It is not true that we came up from the slime and the beast through the jungle, and that we pass out into a night of oblivion unlighted by a single star. It is true that *"in the beginning God created the heavens and the earth"* and that He made *"man in His own image."*

It is true that we came from God through the garden, and that we are destined by obedience to Him to an eternity of joy in a land that is fairer than day, where we will meet again our loved ones who went before, and upon whose blissful shore there falls no shadow and rests no stain.

Again, we irrevocably state that a person cannot claim biblical Christianity and at the same time believe in paganistic evolution, and there is no other type of evolution but that which is paganistic.

(The author is grateful to John Roach Straton for most of the material given above regarding evolution.)

THE BLESSING OF GOD

"And God blessed them, saying, Be fruitful and multiply, and fill the waters in the seas, and let fowl multiply in the earth" (Gen. 1:22).

This presents God doing something different. He blesses His creation of fish and fowls.

It may be asked why God did not bless the plant life. Of them, Moses simply says that God saw that it was good, but He did not bless them; however, here, God begins a new way of propagation, namely, that from living bodies come forth other similar living bodies, which is not true of trees and plants. The pear tree, for example, does not bring forth another pear tree, but only a pear, while a bird produces a bird and a fish a fish. Here, then, is a new creative work, for a living body propagates others out of itself. This indeed is a very marvelous propagation, and there is a marvelous fertility in both the fish and the fowl, especially in the creatures living in the sea.

As humans, when we bless, we can do little more than wish something or someone good, but the blessing of God means propagation. His blessing is just as powerful to propagate as His curse is to cut off.

THE FIFTH DAY

"And the evening and the morning were the fifth day" (Gen. 1:23). This proclaims the creation of sea life and bird life.

THE CREATION OF ANIMALS

"And God said, Let the earth bring forth the living creature after his kind, cattle, and creeping thing, and beast of the earth after his kind: and it was so" (Gen. 1:24).
Verse 24 proclaims the fact that God leaves nothing empty that He has made but furnishes all with His store and riches.

Thus, when He had created the heavens, He furnished them with stars, the air with birds, the water with fish, and the earth with herbs, and plants, and now with beasts and men. So, the earth is full of His riches, and so is the wide sea.

Understanding that, we should realize that God, likewise, will not leave His children empty—the vessels that he has formed for Himself. He desires to fill us with Himself!

Inasmuch as God has created the animal world, we should regard it with appreciation. If we imagine that a tree has as much claim to our attention and regard as a horse, this should not be the case. The latter has a spirit; it possesses animate life. It is a nobler embodiment of divine power.

Even though it is biblically proper for certain animals to be used as food, and, as well, for the skin of certain animals to be used for clothing, etc., still, man must show kindness toward the animal kingdom. Men should never manifest an angry spirit toward them. The brute world was designed by God for the use of man, and it renders its high service in the gift of its life for the sustentation of the human family. The merciful man will be merciful to his beast.

IT IS GOOD

"And God made the beast of the earth after his kind, and cattle after their kind, and everything that creeps upon the earth after his kind: and God saw that it was good" (Gen. 1:25).

This tells us unequivocally that God designed each species of the animal kingdom in such a way that it cannot be crossed.

The difference between the creation of beasts and man cannot be passed over without special observation. Man's body was indeed taken out of the earth, as well as the bodies of the beast, but his soul was not from the earth but from heaven. However, in the creation of beasts, the body and soul, or life, is wholly out of the earth, for the earth is commanded to bring forth the living creatures, that is, the creature with the life thereof. So we find no origination of the soul, or life of the beast, but from the earth only.

As well, there is every evidence that before the fall, or at least as God originally created the animal kingdom, all were plant eaters, which means that none were carnivorous. The fall seemed to have drastically changed some of the animals and turned them into killing machines. More than likely, at the fall the entirety of the animal kingdom was changed some way, and all in a negative sense. Not knowing or seeing the animal kingdom before that time, we really have little knowledge of what they must have been like, except a hint here and there given us in the Word of God.

For instance, it is believed that before the fall, the serpent had the power of limited speech and could even reason somewhat.

We do know this: When the Bible gives the account of him speaking to Eve in the garden of Eden, which was actually at the time of the fall, with Satan using the body of the serpent, Eve didn't seem surprised that the animal could speak (Gen. 3:1–2). If this reptile could speak, is it possible that other animals had such limited power as well?

Also, we find in the book of Isaiah, as the prophet records the coming kingdom age, that the animal kingdom will revert back to its spirit and form before the fall. We find they all once again become plant eaters and that all are now docile (Isa. 11:6–8).

When the latter part of Verse 25 speaks of the creation of the animal kingdom, and that *"God saw that it was good,"* to be sure, the creation at that dawn of time was completely different than what we see presently. The fall affected the animal kingdom terribly so, even though they had no conscious part in this debacle, unless such blame is to be placed on the serpent.

Paul said: *"For the creature was made subject to vanity* (the fall)*, not willingly* (it was not of their doing) *... For we know that the whole creation groans and travails in pain together until now"* (Rom. 8:20, 22).

And the apostle said, *"Because the creature itself also shall be delivered from the bondage of corruption into the glorious liberty of the children of God"* (Rom. 8:21).

THE CREATION OF MAN

"And God said, Let us make man in our image, after our likeness: and let them have dominion over the fish of the sea, and over the fowl of the air, and over the cattle, and over all the earth, and over every creeping thing that creeps upon the earth" (**Gen. 1:26**).

The creation of man was preceded by a divine consultation.

The pronouns *us* and *our* proclaim the consultation held by the three persons of the divine Trinity, who were one in the creative work.

Man is created in the image of God.

He is created in the likeness of God.

He was given dominion over all the earth and over all that was in the earth.

The phrase, *"And God said,"* presents the eighth of the 10 times this phrase is used in Chapters 1 and 2, nine times in Chapter 1 and one time in Chapter 2. These last three times have to do with man exclusively.

The phrase, *"Let us make man,"* proclaims, I think I can say without fear of contradiction, the greatest creative act of God. Actually, the very name *Adam,* at least from the Arabic root, signifies "the brilliant one." Due to the fact that man was created in the image of God and in His likeness, it tells us that man was originally created greater than the angels.

David said:

> *When I consider Your heavens, the work of Your fingers, the moon and the stars, which You have ordained; What is man, that You are mindful of him? and the son of man, that You visit him? For You have made him a little lower than the angels, and have crowned him with glory and honor. You made him to have dominion over the works of Your hands; You have put all things under his feet* (Ps. 8:3–6).

CHRIST AND MAN

As the Holy Spirit asked the question through David concerning man, both the question and the answer concern Christ. In other words, it's speaking of the incarnation of Christ. But yet, due to the fact that Christ is *"the Man,"* it answers for man in general also.

Verse 5 of Psalm 8 was translated, *"For You have made him a little lower than the angels."* It should have been translated, *"You have made him a little lower than the Godhead."* The Hebrew word translated *angels* is *Elohim* and means "God."

As well, God gave man a form of creative powers. While he is not able to create out of nothing as God can do, still, he is able to take that which God has already made and fashion it into many and varied things. In this, he is given a sense of autonomy and independence, which angels do not seem to have. Therefore, being made or created a little lower than God (Elohim), he is greater than the angels, etc.

As well, the pronoun *us* proclaims the Trinity, even as the word *God,* i.e., "Elohim."

Regarding the creation of man, a divine counsel was called, which consisted of the three persons of the Trinity—God the Father, God the Son, and God the Holy Spirit. When man was made, he was to be dedicated to the Father, the Son, and the Holy Spirit. In fact, it is into that great name that we are baptized, for to that great name we owe our being.

Matthew Henry says, "The three persons of the sacred Trinity at first concurred in counsel and operation in forming man, as afterwards in his recovery from the fall."[5]

A GREAT DIFFERENCE

All of this indicates that there is a great difference between man and all other creatures. Man has much in common with the animals that live with him, eat the same food, and sleep and rest as he does, but here Moses shows that man is a creature that excels all animals.

Then, going to the other end of the spectrum, the Scripture tells us that man will judge angels (I Cor. 6:3).

Of all the things that God has created, as far as we know, man is His last creation. This was done on the sixth day of the bringing of the earth back to a habitable state.

Let's review:

- Day one: God dispelled the darkness with light.

- Day two: God brought about the firmament, which separated the water, by putting some on earth and some in the clouds and creating an expanse between the two.

- Day three: God made the seas and continents of dry land, and plant life was restored.

- Day four: God regulated the sun, moon, and stars.

- Day five: sea life and bird life were brought forth.

- Day six: animal life was created, and then man was created.

- Day seven: God rested on this day, signifying the rest that we have in Christ.

THE CREATION OF MAN

It is true that man's body was formed out of the dust, and thus, it is the same as the forms of the mineral, vegetable, and animal creations.

In fact, as Oken says, the whole animal world is repeated and represented in man. One might even say that the animal kingdom is man broken up into fragments.

However, human nature is not to be despised, for though the human body takes all nature into it, it does so to make it a temple for the worship and service of God. That God designed such a view of the human frame is evident from the fact of the incarnation. Jesus entered the human body and purified it for His indwelling, making it, in a sense, a palace for the divine glory and a shrine for the divine worship.

Concerning the human body, Paul said: *"Know you not that you are the temple of God, and that the Spirit of God dwells in you? If any man defile the temple of God, him shall God destroy; for the temple of God* (human body) *is holy, which temple you are"* (I Cor. 3:16–17).

In fact, Jesus was the first one to refer to the human body as a temple of God. He said, *"Destroy this temple* (speaking of Himself), *and in three days I will raise it up"* (Jn. 2:19–21).

While it is admitted that the human body is the weakest link in the makeup of man regarding spirit, soul, and body, still, the Holy Spirit through Paul told us to *"present your bodies a living sacrifice, holy, acceptable unto God, which is your reasonable service"* (Rom. 12:1).

Paul also said that we are *"waiting for the adoption, to wit, the redemption of our body,"* which refers to the coming resurrection when the human body will then be glorified (Rom. 8:23).

The human body is the weakest link, at least at the present, simply because it has been greatly weakened by the fall. Where man, before the fall, was intended to be guided by his spirit, which was in constant communion with God, because of the fall, he is now guided by the senses (five senses). Due to human nature being corrupted through the fall, every bent of the senses is toward sin. In fact, the sin nature controls unredeemed man. (The sin nature is human nature corrupted.)

Upon coming to Christ, everything changes, with the person becoming a new creation (II Cor. 5:17). The spirit of man is once again in contact with the Spirit of God. In fact, the Holy Spirit literally comes into the human body and mind, making it His temple, as we've already stated (I Cor. 3:16).

But yet, the sin nature remains in the believer, even as Paul explains in Romans, Chapter 6. Due to being born again, we are dead to the sin nature, but it doesn't say that the sin nature itself is dead. In fact, it is very much alive, and due to the fact that it is very much alive, this is where the problem commences.

THE CROSS

If the believer doesn't understand God's prescribed order of victory, in other words, how to live this Christian life, he will try to do it the wrong way, even as Romans, Chapter 7, outlines. This guarantees failure and the ascendancy of the sin nature once again. In fact, this is the great struggle of the Christian.

There is only one way that the believer can maintain ascendancy over the sin nature, in other words, the divine nature ruling rather than the sin nature (II Pet. 1:4). If the believer doesn't function God's way, his situation will be, *"O wretched man that I am! Who shall deliver me from the body of this death?"* (Rom. 7:24).

In fact, Romans, Chapter 7, is the example of the believer attempting to live for God but trying to do so in the wrong way. It is Paul's own personal experience.

PAUL

After Paul was saved and baptized with the Holy Spirit, and even called to be an apostle, which means that at the time in question, he was an apostle, not knowing the victory of the Cross, he set out to live for God in the only way he knew. That way was the effort of trying to live for God by his own strength and ability, which he came to refer to as *"the flesh."*

In his defense, there was no one else in the world at that time who knew of the victory of the Cross, for the explanation of the new covenant had not yet been given. In fact, it was given to Paul. Actually, the explanation of the Cross is the explanation of the new covenant. To simplify the issue, one need only look at the emblems of the Lord's Supper (I Cor. 11:24–25).

So, if the great Paul couldn't live this life by his own strength, how do you think you can?

GOD'S PRESCRIBED ORDER OF VICTORY

The Lord has devised a means and a way for the believer to live a holy, pure, and godly life, meaning that sin will not have dominion over him (Rom. 6:14). As stated, it is the victory of the Cross, which refers to what Jesus did there.

Some have said that all revelation is preceded by desperation. Perhaps that is true. I know it was with Paul, and I know it was with me as well!

The Lord gave to the apostle this prescribed order, which he gave to us in Romans, Chapter 6. Someone has well said that Romans, Chapter 6, is the mechanics of the Holy Spirit, which tells us how He works. Romans, Chapter 8, is the dynamics of the Holy Spirit, which tells us what He does after we understand how He does it.

The apostle explained to us that at the time of conversion, we are literally baptized into the death of Christ. Now, of course, we were not there when Jesus was crucified; however, when the believing sinner evidences faith in Christ, in the mind of God, Jesus Christ becomes our substitute in all things. When He died, we died with Him and were literally baptized into His death (Rom. 6:3). This is all done by faith on our part. In other words, when the sinner expresses faith in Christ, we are placed by God into the death of Christ.

Now, please understand that when Paul said that we are baptized into His death, he was not speaking of water baptism, as many think. He was speaking of the crucifixion of Christ, but it didn't stop there; it continues.

Paul then said, *"Therefore we are buried with Him by baptism into death,"* meaning that when Jesus was put in the tomb, in the mind of God, we were placed in that tomb with Him. This means that all of the old man is not only *"crucified with Him, that the body of sin might be destroyed,"* but buried with Him, meaning that the old you is gone forever (Rom. 6:4, 6).

However, it doesn't stop there. When Christ was raised from the dead by the glory of the Father, we were raised with Him that *"we also should walk in newness of life"* (Rom. 6:4–5).

This which I've just explained to you is the bedrock of the Christian faith. It is what Christ did for us at the Cross and is the very reason that Paul also said, *"But God forbid that I should glory, save in the Cross of our Lord Jesus Christ, by whom the world is crucified unto me, and I unto the world"* (Gal. 6:14).

The believer is to ever understand that everything he receives from God comes to him exclusively by and through the Cross of Christ. While everything that Christ did is of utmost significance, still, it is what He did at the Cross that redeemed us. In other words, we live *"in the likeness of His resurrection"* only as we understand that *"we have been planted together* (Christ and ourselves) *in the likeness of His death"* (Rom. 6:5).

THE OBJECT OF OUR FAITH

The idea is that the Cross of Christ must ever be the object of our faith. This is so very, very important! While everything that God has and does is, of necessity, of vast significance, still, it is what He did at the Cross for us, by the giving of

His only Son, that *"deliver(ed) us from this present evil world"* (Jn. 3:16; Gal. 1:4).

In fact, the Holy Spirit works exclusively within the parameters of the finished work of Christ. Paul tells us that in Romans 8:2. He said, *"For the law* (a law made by the Godhead) *of the Spirit of life* (Holy Spirit) *in Christ Jesus* (what Jesus did at the Cross) *has made me free from the law of sin and death"* (The Expositor's Study Bible).

The words *"in Christ Jesus"* tell us how the Spirit of God works within our lives. In other words, all that He does for us, to us, in us, and of us is done totally and completely within the parameters of the sacrifice of Christ, which gives Him the legal right to do these great things. There's only one law in this world that is greater than the law of sin and death, and that is the law of the Spirit of life in Christ Jesus. In fact, Paul uses this term *"in Christ Jesus,"* or one of its derivatives, such as *"in Him,"* etc., 170 times in his 14 epistles. More than any other short phrase, the words *"in Christ Jesus"* define the Christian faith.

FAITH

The Holy Spirit is the only one who can help us to live this life as we should. For Him to work within our lives and to do so on a constant basis, which alone guarantees us victory, we must evidence faith in Christ and what Christ did at the Cross. Paul said, *"Likewise reckon you also yourselves to be dead indeed unto sin* (dead unto the sin nature), *but alive unto God through Jesus Christ our Lord* (what He did for us at the Cross)"* (Rom. 6:11).

We are to reckon ourselves, or to account ourselves, according to what Jesus did at the Cross. We are to understand that He did it all for us, and for us exclusively, and that when He died, we died with Him, were buried with Him, and were raised with Him in newness of life (Rom. 6:3–5).

When this is done, we have the promise that *"sin shall not have dominion over you: for you are not under the law* (that having been satisfied by Christ at the Cross), *but under grace"* (Rom. 6:14; Col. 2:14–15).

THE METHOD

Perhaps the following, which abbreviates all that I have just said, will be of some help. To live a holy life, this is what the Christian must continually do:

- We must understand that Jesus Christ is the source of all things that we receive from God (Jn. 1:1-3, 14, 29; 14:6, 20).

- We must understand that the Cross of Christ is the means by which all of these wonderful things are given to us. In other words, it's the Cross that made it possible (Rom. 6:1-14; I Cor. 1:17, 18, 23; 2:2; Gal. 6:14).

- Understand that Jesus is the source, the Cross is the means, and the object of our faith must be Jesus Christ and Him crucified (Col. 2:10-15).

- Understand that Christ is the source, the Cross is the means, the Cross of Christ is the object of our faith, and that the Holy Spirit, who works exclusively within the parameters of the finished work of Christ, i.e., the Cross, will work mightily on our behalf. The Holy Spirit is God, and that means He can do anything. However, we must not forget that He works exclusively through and by the Cross of Christ. So, this means that our faith must ever rest in Christ and the Cross (Rom. 8:1-11; Eph. 2:13-18).

THE KEY

Faith is the key to the great treasure house of God. Most every Christian would agree with that statement; however, beyond that simple statement, most have very little understanding. In other words, most Christians don't have the foggiest clue how to put faith to work.

I suppose that if most Christians had to give a definition of what we're talking about here, their minds would go to various Scriptures, thinking that quoting them by rote would somehow generate faith, etc.

While quoting the Word of God is always good, that within itself, at least as we have stated it, will never build faith. While faith definitely *"comes by hearing, and hearing by the Word of God"* (Rom. 10:17), we must know what that means for it to be effective within our lives.

To make it brief, we must understand that the Word of God is actually the story of man's redemption. This redemption was carried out by the Lord Jesus Christ and what He did at the Cross. That's why Paul said, *"We preach Christ crucified"* (I Cor. 1:23).

FAITH ANCHORED IN CHRIST

In the gospel according to John, we are told:

- *"In the beginning was the Word, and the Word was with God, and the Word was God"* (Jn. 1:1). This tells us that Jesus is the living Word.

- John said, *"And the Word was made flesh, and dwelt among us"* (Jn. 1:14). This speaks of the incarnation, and then we are told what the incarnation was all about.

- Then, as he introduced Christ, the apostle said, *"Behold the Lamb of God, which takes away the sin of the world"* (Jn. 1:29).

In abbreviated form, we have here the total picture of the Word of God. We are introduced to Christ, who is the living Word. We are told that this Word was made flesh. We are then told what it was all about, which was the Cross.

So, our faith must be anchored in Christ, but for it to be properly anchored in Christ, we must understand that it is Christ crucified. We must never separate Christ from His finished work or the finished work from Christ. Of course, we know that Jesus is no longer on the Cross. In fact, He is presently in heaven, seated by the right hand of the Father (Eph. 2:6; Heb. 1:3). What we are actually talking about are the results of the Cross.

The total meaning of the crucifixion is something that happened in the past, was done so well that it will never have to be repeated, and has continued results. In fact, the results will never be discontinued. It's those results of which we speak.

It's like the Constitution of the United States. We don't go back and rewrite the Constitution constantly, but we do constantly enjoy its benefits.

It is the same with the Cross! It does not have to be repeated because what Jesus did there will eternally suffice. That's the reason that Paul referred to it as *"the everlasting covenant"* (Heb. 13:20).

So, when we speak of faith, we must always understand that Christ and His Cross must ever be the object of our faith. If it's not faith in Christ and what He did for us at the Cross, then it's faith that God will not recognize.

In this manner and this manner alone—and I speak of functioning according to God's prescribed order of victory, which is the Cross—can the believer live a victorious, overcoming, Christian life. In this manner alone can the human body be a proper temple, overcoming every power of darkness (Eph. 2:13–18; Col. 2:10–15).

FAITH IN THE CROSS

That's the reason that we must never allow anything else, no matter how holy it might be in its own right, to come between us and our faith in the Cross. Concerning this, Paul said, *"For Christ sent me not to baptize, but to preach the gospel: not with wisdom of words, lest the Cross of Christ should be made of none effect"* (I Cor. 1:17).

Was Paul denigrating water baptism? No, he wasn't! He was merely stating that we must not allow anything to be preeminent, in other words, to take the place of the Cross.

FALLEN FROM GRACE

If we do this, the apostle then says, *"Christ shall profit you nothing"* (Gal. 5:2).

We must remember that Paul was speaking to believers. He plainly tells us in Chapter 5 of Galatians that if we place other things ahead of the Cross, claiming those other things as the way to victory, *"Christ is become of no effect unto you"* (Gal. 5:4).

That's the terrible problem that affixes itself to most Christians. They are trusting in things other than the Cross, making Christ of no effect. This guarantees spiritual failure. In fact, when the believers do this, they fall from grace. In other words, the goodness of God, which, in effect, is the grace of God, can no longer be extended to such Christians. The end result of such a position is bleak indeed!

However, if the Christian doesn't understand the Cross, which means that he is placing his faith in other things, the grace of God simply cannot come to him. In other words, as Paul also said, such a position *"frustrate(s) the grace of God"* (Gal. 2:21). The sadness is, most Christians know almost nothing about the

Cross. Actually, almost all Christians think they do, but the truth is, they don't! As a result, they are trying to live this life in all the wrong ways, which frustrates the grace of God and guarantees failure.

When the focus of Christians is on works, with the object of faith being their performance, which means the power source is self, this guarantees defeat.

Total and complete trust in Christ and what Christ has done for us at the Cross guarantees a continued flow of the grace of God, which guarantees victory. There is no other way, as there doesn't need to be any other way.

IMAGE AND LIKENESS

The phrase, *"In Our image, after Our likeness,"* refers to true righteousness and holiness.

Ephesians 4:24 says, *"And that you put on the new man, which after God is created in righteousness and true holiness."*

The Pulpit Commentary says that the precise relationship in which the nature of the *"Adam"* about to be created should stand to *"Elohim"* was to be that of a *tselem,* which means "shadow." It denotes the shadowy outline of a figure.[6]

The image and likeness also enable us to have fellowship with God, but it does not mean we are gods or can become gods. We were created dependent beings (Ps. 8:5), and even in the new heavens and the new earth, we shall continue to be dependent on the light and energy that God provides through Christ as we both serve God and reign with Christ (Rev. 21:23; 22:3–5).

Man created in the image and likeness of God makes him totally different from the animal creation and, in fact, light years ahead of that creation in every capacity. The Bible nowhere links man with animals. In fact, man is not an animal. He is a human being, created, as stated, in the image and likeness of God. This is not said about any of God's other creations. In fact, we blaspheme when we put man in the category of animals because in so doing, we have placed God in the same category.

EXACTLY HOW IS MAN IN THE IMAGE AND LIKENESS OF GOD?

Man created in the image and likeness of God pertains to the spiritual and not the physical. In fact, the human body is but a tent or a tabernacle that houses the soul and the spirit, which are indestructible and eternal. While the human body is to be looked at as a temple, even as we've already explained, it is the least of man's triune makeup of spirit, soul, and body (I Thess. 5:23).

This image and likeness of God in man, and created that way, pertain to man's ability to reason, to love, and to serve. These amazing faculties were meant to function entirely in the realm of service to our Creator. In this image and likeness, man is given an amazing degree of latitude. He was created as a free moral agent, but the fall ruined all of this. Man died spiritually, and as such, at the fall, he lost the image and likeness of God.

We must understand that at the fall, man was not merely wounded in a spiritual sense, or even wounded severely.

Spiritually, he died, and we must not forget that dead is dead. This means that man has nothing left in him that pertains to God. He has fallen all the way from total God-consciousness down to the far lower level of total self-consciousness. As a result, he has little regard for others, only that for himself.

MORALITY

Some preachers misunderstand what seems to be morality evidenced in the lives of unbelievers. However, let all know and understand that any and all morality shown in the doings of unbelievers is strictly from the influence of biblical Christianity. If one looks at the nations of the world that have had little teaching regarding biblical Christianity, one will find that interest is shown in others only as it benefits self-interest.

For the spiritual connection of man to once again be reestablished with God, man must be born again. Jesus said: *"Except a man be born again, he cannot see the kingdom of God"* (Jn. 3:3). For this great work to be carried out in man, a tremendous plan had to be put into effect, in fact, a plan that originated even before the foundation of the world (I Pet. 1:18–20).

God would have to become man, which He did, and literally die on a Cross in order for the terrible problem of sin to be properly addressed. When Jesus died on the Cross, He addressed every single thing that man lost in the fall. Admittedly, at the present, we only have the firstfruits of that which Jesus did, with the balance coming at the resurrection; however, we must never forget that it took the Cross to address the situation.

Only through faith in Christ and what He did at the Cross, all on our behalf, can we regain what was lost—the image and likeness of God.

DOMINION

"And let them have dominion over the fish of the sea, and over the fowl of the air, and over the cattle, and over all the earth, and over every creeping thing that creeps upon the earth" (Gen. 1:26).

This proclaims two things:

1. This dominion was given by God to man.

2. The relationship of man to the rest of creation is now defined to be one of rule and supremacy. The sphere of his lordship is from the lowest to the highest of the subjects placed beneath his sway.

Incidentally, the word *man* in this verse actually means "mankind"; hence, the word *them.*

This dominion that God gave unto man was meant to be carried on in a responsible way; however, the fall, while not taking away this dominion, did cause man to warp and twist that which God intended.

Once again, even in this enlightened age, when you go to the nations of the world that little know God, you find a rape of the land and the resources, irrespective of what kind, to be appalling!

DOMINION AND SELF

When we carry the word *dominion* to its full length, it should be understood that it is dominion under God; however, as a free moral agent, man could do with this dominion what he liked.

The fall resulted in Satan gaining a dominion over man, which means that man has lost the greater part of this dominion. Satan is now *"the god of this world* (who) *has blinded the minds of them which believe not, lest the light of the glorious gospel of Christ, who is the image of God, should shine unto them"* (II Cor. 4:4).

At the fall, man lost dominion over self, which means that he is no longer ruled by God, but rather by his own passions, and passions, we might quickly say, that are evil. That's why Paul constantly spoke of our own personal strength and efforts as *"the flesh"* (Rom. 8:1, 8).

As someone has rightly said, "When Jesus died on the Cross, He did so not only to save us from sin but, as well, to save us from self." The only way that dominion over self, which is the first requirement of all, can be regained is by the person first of all being born again and then continuing to look exclusively to the Cross for all things.

That's what Jesus was talking about when He said: *"If any man will come after Me, let him deny himself, and take up his Cross daily, and follow Me. For whosoever will save his life shall lose it: but whosoever will lose his life for My sake, the same shall save it"* (Lk. 9:23–24).

TAKING UP THE CROSS DAILY

Most Christians misunderstand this statement made by Christ.

When He spoke of denying self, He wasn't speaking of asceticism, which is the denial of all things that are pleasurable or comfortable. He was speaking of denying self in the capacity of our own strength and ability, meaning that we understand that we cannot live this life by our own means. We can only do so as Christ lives through us.

When He spoke of taking up the Cross daily and following Him, He wasn't meaning suffering, as most Christians think. He was meaning that every single blessing we receive from the Lord—every good thing—all and without exception, come through the finished work of Christ on the Cross. Consequently, even on a daily basis, we are to draw down these benefits of what Jesus did at the Cross. That's the way we live and maintain our victory.

When He spoke of saving our lives and, thereby, losing them, He was meaning that if we try to live for God by our own machinations and ability, instead of saving our lives, we will actually lose them. However, when we lose our lives for His sake, meaning that we give it all to Him and trust completely in what Christ did at the Cross on our behalf, then we save our lives. It's just that simple! It is all in Christ, and if it's not in Christ, there is no proper dominion over self.

Paul said, *"I am crucified with Christ: nevertheless I live; yet not I, but Christ lives in me: and the life which I now live in the flesh I live by the faith of the Son of God, who loved me, and gave Himself for me"* (Gal. 2:20).

MALE AND FEMALE

"So God created man in His own image, in the image of God created He him; male and female created He them" (Gen. 1:27).

As far as we know, this represents the first time that God has created the female gender, at least as it regards intelligent beings. There is no record of any female angels.

The threefold repetition of the word *created* should be observed as a distinct rebuttal against the mindless philosophy of evolution.

Evolution teaches that man is gradually evolving into something better and better, while creationism teaches that man has rather fallen from his high beginning.

As well, the Holy Spirit here through Moses not only speaks of creation some three times, but, also, some three times He makes mention of man created in the image of God. As stated, that image, however, was lost at the fall.

MARTIN LUTHER

Martin Luther said the following, which I repeat:

But now it is the purpose of the gospel to restore this divine image. By faith we are born again unto eternal life, or let me rather say, to the hope of eternal life, so that we live in God and with Him, and are one with Him, as Christ says. But we are not only born again unto eternal life, but also unto righteousness, for our faith receives the merit of Christ, as we steadfastly believe that we are ransomed through His death. To this must be added another righteousness or image of God, according to which, instructed by the divine Word, we diligently try, with the help of the Holy Spirit, to render obedience to God. But this righteousness merely begins in this life; because of the corruption of our nature it can never become perfect. Yet God is pleased with it, not as though it were perfect or an atonement for our sin, but because it flows from a sincere heart, which, endowed by faith, trusts in God's mercy for Christ's sake.

Through the gospel we receive also the Holy Spirit, who wars against the unbelief, envy and other vices in us and makes us earnestly strive to honor God and His Word. Thus there begins in this life the restoration of the divine image through the gospel, though this is never fully accomplished here upon earth. But when it will be accomplished in the heavenly kingdom of God, then our will shall be perfectly free from sin, and perfectly good, and our intellect will be perfectly enlightened, and the memory will be absolutely unfailing.

THE BLESSING OF GOD

"And God blessed them, and God said unto them, Be fruitful, and multiply, and replenish the earth, and subdue it: and have

dominion over the fish of the sea, and over the fowl of the air, and over every living thing that moves upon the earth" (Gen. 1:28).

This proclaims the blessing of God, which is the very opposite of the curse.

In the word *multiply,* we have the meaning of procreation.

When God created the angels, every evidence is that He created all of them at the same time. In other words, there's never been such a thing as a baby angel. However, when He created mankind, He created them male and female and gave them the power of procreation, which refers to the ability to bring offspring into the world.

In fact, it was the intention of God that these offspring would be sons of God, and, thereby, continue in the image of God; however, the fall ruined that in that offspring now are brought into the world in the likeness of Adam, with all of its attendant misery, and not like God (Gen. 5:3).

REPLENISH

The word *replenish* is thought by some to point to a former creation on the earth before Adam and Eve.

According to Isaiah, Chapter 14, and Ezekiel, Chapter 28, Lucifer ruled this world for an undetermined period of time, and did so in righteousness and holiness as a beautiful angel created by God. This was in the dateless past, as stated, before Adam and Eve.

If, in fact, he did rule this world at that time, it would stand to reason that there had to be some type of creation on the earth for him to rule. Some believe that the word *replenish* is referring to that creation.

When Lucifer fell, this creation, whatever it was, threw in its lot with him, as did approximately one-third of the angels. In fact, some think that demon spirits are actually the spirits of this fallen creation. One thing is certain: Demon spirits aren't fallen angels. Fallen angels have spirit bodies, and demon spirits have no bodies at all, but seek to inhabit a body, whether animal or man.

As is obvious, the Bible doesn't give us much information on this inasmuch as the Bible is the story of the creation, fall, and redemption of man and not angels, etc. But yet, what little it does say in this respect lends credence to the idea of what we have just stated.

FOOD

"And God said, Behold, I have given you every herb bearing seed, which is upon the face of all the earth, and every tree, in the which is the fruit of a tree yielding seed; to you it shall be for meat. And to every beast of the earth, and to every fowl of the air, and to every thing that creeps upon the earth, wherein there is life, I have given every green herb for meat: and it was so," (Gen. 1:29-30).

This passage refers to the fact that both animals and mankind were vegetarians before the fall. Incidentally, this was changed after the flood (Gen. 9:3).

Of the three classes into which the vegetable creation was divided—grass, herbs, and trees—the last two were assigned to man for food.

We are told in Verse 30 that the green grass was given to the animal kingdom for food. The phrase, *"Every beast of the earth, and to every fowl of the air, and to every thing that creeps upon the earth,"* tells us that the animals were not originally created as predators.

In other words, all animals were then vegetarian, as well, which means that all, and not just some, were docile.

That means that the lamb and the lion played together exactly as they will do again in the coming kingdom age (Isa. 11:6–8).

VERY GOOD

"And God saw every thing that He had made, and, behold, it was very good. And the evening and the morning were the sixth day" (Gen. 1:31).

This means that it was not simply good, but good exceedingly. It is not man alone that God surveys but the completed cosmos, with man as its crown and glory.

By using such terminology, God has hereby set us an example of reviewing our works. Having given us a power of reflection, He expects that we should use that power. When we have finished a day's work and are entering upon the rest of the night, we should commune with our own hearts about what we have done that day.

However, when we come to review our works, we find so often that to our shame, much has been very bad; but when God reviewed His work, all was very good.

THE SIXTH DAY

In six days, God brought the world back to a habitable state, plus He created plant life, the animal kingdom, and mankind.

From this, we are not to think that God couldn't have perfected this work in a much shorter period of time. Actually, due to the fact that He is almighty and all-knowing, He could have spoken it into existence in a moment's time. However, He did it in this way, taking some six days, in order that we might see His wisdom, power, goodness, and order.

We find from this that God's government extends even to His creation, and above all to His creation. Government demands order, and God's order is perfect, thereby, meaning that His government is perfect as well.

Matthew Henry said, and I concur, "Thus ends a chapter containing the most extensive, the most profound, and most sublime truths that can possibly come within the reach of the human understanding."[7]

———•◆•———

We praise Thee, O God, our Redeemer, Creator,
In grateful devotion our tribute we bring.
We lay it before Thee, we kneel and adore Thee.
We bless Thy holy name, glad praises we sing.

We worship Thee, God of our fathers, we bless Thee;
Through life's storm and tempest our guide hast Thou been.
When perils overtake us, escape Thou wilt make us,
And with Your help, O Lord, our battles we win.

With voices united our praises we offer,
To Thee, great Jehovah, glad anthems we raise.
Your strong arm will guide us, our God is beside us,
To Thee, our great Redeemer, forever be praised.

the fall of man

CHAPTER 2

THE CREATION OF MAN

THE CREATION OF MAN

"THUS THE HEAVENS AND the earth were finished, and all the host of them" (Gen. 2:1).

THE HEAVENS AND THE EARTH ARE FINISHED

This proclaims the fact that when the heavens and the earth were completed, they were a brilliant array.

I think one can say without fear of any scriptural contradiction that everything, including the heavens, was affected negatively in some way as a result of the fall. In fact, Paul said in relation to this, *"For we know that the whole creation groans and travails in pain together until now"* (Rom. 8:22).

So, as beautiful as the heavens are presently, how must they have looked before the fall? As far as our ability to view what presently is there, even that has been greatly impeded in this industrial age.

In the early 1970s, Frances and I, along with Donnie and Debbie and others, were in South Africa in a series of meetings.

At the conclusion of the meetings, we had two or three days' layover, which we spent at the Kruger Game Preserve, one of the largest in the world.

I remember that on the first night we were there, I walked outside the little hut in which we were staying and looked up at the stars. It was something I had never seen in all of my life.

It seemed as if the heavens were literally blanketed with stars. Because of the pollution in the air back in the states, I had not seen anything of this nature. For nearly an hour I suppose, I stood there mesmerized, looking at this carpet of stars in the heavens, which was so beautiful as to be beyond description.

So, if one can think back in his imagination to before the fall, the heavens at that time must have been an array of unimagined beauty. They will be that way again. John the Beloved said, *"And I saw a new heaven and a new earth: for the first heaven and the first earth were passed away; and there was no more sea"* (Rev. 21:1).

FINISHED

When the Lord said that the creation, or possibly one should say, the re-creation, was finished, all was pristine and beautiful beyond compare. About 4,000 years later, while hanging on a cruel Cross, His Son would again say, *"It is finished,"* and the way back to God was then open, but what a price had to be paid! In fact, it was such a price as to make the original creation seem as if it were nothing. As beautiful as material things might be, they are still just things; however, the Son of God gave His life on that Cross, and nothing can equal that.

On a coming day, the final words will then be said, *"It is done"* (Rev. 21:6). In fact, this will be after the millennial reign when the new heaven and the new earth will be brought into being. Then, Satan and all of his cohorts of darkness will be placed in the lake of fire forever and forever, and sin will be only a bad memory, if that.

THE SEVENTH DAY

"And on the seventh day God ended His work which He had made; and He rested on the seventh day from all His work which He had made" (Gen. 2:2).

This presents an anthropomorphic statement. In other words, it's a statement made about God in the ways and manner of men so that we might understand it better. God cannot be conceived as resting or as needing rest through either exhaustion or fatigue. The prophet said of Him that He *"faints not, neither is weary"* (Isa. 40:28). Cessation from previous occupation is all that is implied in this statement.

Incidentally, a morning here for the Sabbath day is implied, but no evening as with the other days is implied. The Sabbath is actually eternal. It foretells Christ, the true Sabbath, in whom God rests and in whom believers rest. This is God's own rest of Hebrews, Chapter 4.

When it says that God *"rested on the seventh day from all His work which He had made,"* I think we can derive from this phrase that He is not creating new universes. Since that time, He has given Himself to the new work of upholding His creation. The Scripture says, *"By Him* (Christ) *all things consist"* (Col. 1:17).

Since the fall of man in the garden of Eden, God has given Himself to the carrying out of the plan of redemption. Concerning this, Jesus said, *"My Father worketh hitherto, and I work"* (Jn. 5:17). That's the reason that beginning with Genesis, Chapter 4, and continuing throughout the balance of the Word of God, we have the story of man's redemption. The whole of this recorded past—6,000 years—has been spent in this process.

BLESSING

"And God blessed the seventh day, and sanctified it: because that in it He had rested from all His work which God created and made" (Gen. 2:3).

This presents the third blessing. Williams said: "Blessing is stamped upon this introduction to the history of God's interest in man and His creatures. He blessed the living creatures (Gen. 1:22); He blessed man (Gen. 1:28), and He now blesses the seventh day."[1]

If we fail here to see what the Lord is actually doing, then we will miss completely the import of what is being said.

This Sabbath, or seventh day (Saturday), the last day of the week, is meant by God to be a type of the salvation rest that one finds in Christ. That's the reason it was a part of the Ten Commandments.

When an individual accepts Christ, he enters into a Sabbath rest so to speak, which will never end. That's the reason no mention is made of an evening and morning for the seventh day. Read carefully what Paul said: *"Let us therefore fear, lest, a promise being left us of entering into His rest, any of you should seem to come short of it"* (Heb. 4:1).

We enter into this rest not by keeping a certain day. That's not what it means at all. If that's what we seek to do, then we will *"come short of it."*

REST

One enters into this rest by accepting Christ and making Him the Lord of one's life. Then Paul said, *"For unto us was the gospel preached, as well as unto them* (Jews before the Cross and Jews after the Cross)*: but the Word preached did not profit them, not being mixed with faith in them who heard it"* (Heb. 4:2).

Paul is saying that the Word preached to the Jews before the Cross did not profit them simply because they tried to make salvation out of the keeping of the Sabbath day. This meant that they had no faith in the one to whom the Sabbath day pointed.

Paul continues, *"For we which have believed do enter into rest, as He said, As I have sworn in My wrath, if they shall enter into My rest: although the works were finished from the foundation of the world"* (Heb. 4:3).

In this Scripture, Paul is saying that all the works of God were finished on the sixth day; consequently, there must not be any more works. We enter into this rest, as stated, not by keeping a certain day, but by accepting the one whom the seventh day typified. Paul said, *"For He spoke in a certain place of the seventh day on this wise, And God did rest the seventh day from all His works"* (Heb. 4:4).

This was spoken in Genesis 2:2. Once again He emphasizes the fact that all the works are now finished. This means that if man tries to find salvation by works or maintain salvation by works, God has sworn in His wrath that man will not enter into His rest by such efforts.

CHRIST AND THE CROSS

The apostle then said, *"For he who is entered into His rest, he also has ceased from his own works, as God did from His"* (Heb. 4:10).

So, we see from all of this that God blessing and sanctifying the seventh day refers strictly to Christ and the rest that He brought us by what He did at the Cross on our behalf. We obtain this rest by exhibiting faith in Him and His great sacrifice. If we try to obtain it any other way, which then places us in the position of works, such activity angers God greatly (Heb. 4:3).

When God finished all His work on the sixth day, and He *"saw everything that He had made, and, behold, it was very good"* (Gen. 1:31), that meant that all work and works were finished. To be sure, even as Paul said in Hebrews, Chapter 4, it pointed to the coming redemption found only in Christ, which can only be obtained by faith and never by works. So, the Sabbath was meant to portray Christ and the great rest that He would afford by what He did for the human race in the offering up of Himself on the Cross. Consequently, the Lord blessing and sanctifying this particular day carries a meaning far greater than the mere fact that He had finished the creation.

THE RESURRECTION OF CHRIST
AND THE FIRST DAY OF THE WEEK

If we are to notice in the book of Acts and the Epistles, the Sabbath, which is Saturday, gradually fell by the wayside, with the first day of the week, the day of the resurrection of Christ, taking its place (Acts 20:7; I Cor. 16:2; Rev. 1:10).

Jesus fulfilled all of the law, which included the Sabbath. As stated, He rose from the dead on the first day of the week, and this was, no doubt, done purposely. It signals not an ending, but rather a beginning. And so it is!

GENERATIONS

"These are the generations of the heavens and of the earth when they were created, in the day that the LORD *God made the earth and the heavens"* (Gen. 2:4).

"These are the generations," occurs 11 times in this first book of the Bible. *Generations* refers to "divine divisions."

The phrase, *"These are the generations of the heavens and of the earth when they were created,"* refers to the manner in which all were created as outlined in Genesis, Chapter 1. As stated, the Lord has an ordered procedure about all that He does. His government is perfect regarding creation, as well as all other things. He is a God of order.

In this government of order, much of the time, one can tell what God is going to do by what He has done in the past. There is no chaos about Him. At the same time, due to man's fallen nature, there is nothing but chaos about him. Consequently, for man to have an ordered existence, he must serve God and, thereby, learn the ways of the Lord that he may walk therein. Only in this manner can man walk in a semblance of order. Otherwise, he has disorder.

One only has to look at the nations of the world that subscribe, at least to a certain extent, to the Bible. This means that they have at least a goodly number of their population who serve the Lord. That nation will be orderly and will prosper. Otherwise, as we have already stated, there is chaos. Someone has well made the following points and rightly so:

- No Bible, no freedom!

- Some Bible, some freedom!

- Much Bible, much freedom!

THE LORD GOD

The phrase, *"In the day that the LORD God made the earth and the heavens,"* presents the new name of God as Jehovah Elohim.

Jehovah is the absolute, self-existent one, who manifests Himself to man, and in particular, enters into distinct covenant engagements for man's redemption, which, in due time, He fulfills.

Concerning this new name, Williams says: "This chapter reveals Christ as Jehovah Elohim, man's Redeemer. The first chapter reveals Him as Elohim, man's Creator. He first prepares the beauteous world in which man is to dwell and then He creates man, and, as Jehovah, enters into covenant with him. These two great titles of Christ are distinguished throughout the entire Bible and finally appear in its two closing chapters, which treat of redeemed man and a new earth."[2]

The words *created* and *made* literally say "created to make." The idea is that God made the world in such a way that it can be almost endlessly developed. This is tied in with man's dominion, which, regrettably, has been at least partially taken over by Satan. Consequently, that which God originally intended, which is a greater development, has been all but halted in its tracks. However, this will be remedied with the coming new heaven and new earth.

THE PLANTS AND THE HERBS

"And every plant of the field before it was in the earth, and every herb of the field before it grew: for the LORD God had not caused it to rain upon the earth, and there was not a man to till the ground" (Gen. 2:5).

The second day of creation is addressed here, which obviously preceded day three when plant life was developed.

It seems that rain came to the earth on day three, which caused the earth to *"bring forth grass, the herb yielding seed, and the fruit tree yielding fruit after his kind"* (Gen. 1:11).

All of this was before man was created, showing that he had nothing to do with the creation, with that being altogether of God.

The phrase, *"And every plant of the field before it was in the earth, and every herb of the field before it grew,"* presents the fact that the earth did not bring forth vegetation of itself—by any innate virtue of its own—but purely by the almighty power of God, who formed every plant and every herb before it grew in the earth.

In these few words, the Holy Spirit is informing all and sundry that creation is altogether of God. This completely debunks evolution and, as well, man's involvement, as we shall see. There is nothing that is created that is a product of man, with God always being the first cause. It is on this one truth that fallen man runs aground. While man can further develop God's creation, which God originally intended, man cannot bring something out of nothing. That domain lies completely in the realm of God.

HUMOROUS STORY

There is a joke of sorts which says that man approached God and informed Him that he (man) was now so brilliant that the services of God were no longer needed.

So, God proposed a little contest, to which man readily agreed. God would create a man, and then it was proposed that man would do the same. Man agreed, thinking he could easily clone a specimen.

God reached down and gathered together a little pile of dirt from which His man would be made. But when man reached down and did the same thing, God asked what he was doing.

"I'm getting a pile of dirt in order to make man exactly as You have done," he replied.

The Lord answered, "Get your own dirt."

RAIN

The phrase, *"For the LORD God had not caused it to rain upon the earth,"* proclaims the fact that there had not yet been any rain, even though God had divided the waters and had put some in clouds and left some on the earth with an expanse between, which was called *"the firmament"* (Gen. 1:6–8).

The insinuation is that God did cause it to rain upon the earth on day three and, thereby, caused the earth to *"bring forth grass, the herb yielding seed,"* etc.

This shows us that all of creation is subject to God, and that God is subject not at all to creation. We must never forget that!

When all the seed in the earth had been placed there by God, and they were properly ready to bud and bring forth, then God caused it to rain.

Even though everything has been somewhat perverted due to the fall, which means that it doesn't quite function properly, still, that which God originally created continues to function exactly as He originally created it to do, with the exception of the perversions. By perversions, we're speaking of droughts, hurricanes, earthquakes, storms, floods, etc. All of these types of things were never intended by God but came into being due to the fall. As we have previously stated, that's the reason *"that the whole creation groans and travails in pain together until now"* (Rom. 8:22).

THE INVOLVEMENT OF MAN

The phrase, *"And there was not a man to till the ground,"* more than anything else, refers to the fact that man had nothing to do with creation. Consequently, man should be very careful about taking credit for anything as it pertains to the works of God. In fact, man is due no credit at all!

When we think of plants growing, we think of man putting seed in the earth and cultivating the ground. Plant life was developed on day three, some three days before man was even created.

To understand these particular words, we must bear in mind that the object of the narrative is not the formation of the world, but man's relation to Jehovah, hence, the introduction of the new name of God—Jehovah Elohim.

Man's proper relationship to God is, in essence, a very simple relationship. In other words, it's not difficult to understand, and if it is complicated, it is that man has complicated the process himself.

We must recognize God as the Creator of all things. As such, we must give Him proper praise and glory. However, due to the fall, man has great problems on both counts.

He doesn't want to recognize God as the Creator, thereby, he substitutes the mindless drivel of evolution to explain creation and, accordingly, refuses to give God praise and glory.

The idea is that if man will not recognize God as Elohim, his Creator, then he will not recognize God as Jehovah Elohim, his Redeemer.

A MIST

"But there went up a mist from the earth, and watered the whole face of the ground" (Gen. 2:6).

This pertains to day two of creation.

At that time (day two), there went up a mist from the earth, which prepared the earth for the seed that God evidently planted on the beginning of day three.

Once again, we see God as the original cause of all creation.

The phrase, *"But there went up a mist from the earth,"* was done, as stated, on day two, which prepared the earth for the seed that was to be applied by God, which the rain would bring forth on day three.

THE GROUND

The phrase, *"And watered the whole face of the ground,"* presents the fact that the earth was made ready for that which would take place the next day.

Some commentators have attempted to use these passages as proof that the days mentioned in Chapter 1 were not literal 24-hour days. However, once it is understood what is actually being said, even as I think we have satisfactorily explained, we are given to understand that the Holy Spirit is portraying here through Moses the manner and the way in which God carried this out, which was done in literal 24-hour days.

THE WAY MAN WAS CREATED

"And the LORD *God formed man of the dust of the ground, and breathed into his nostrils the breath of life; and man became a living soul"* (Gen. 2:7).

Man being formed of the dust of the ground proclaims this physical body of clay. To understand and remember this, such ought to inspire a feeling of genuine humility. It should keep men from pride and reference to their renowned ancestry, their apparel, or their wealth inasmuch as we are the workmanship of His hands and, therefore, must not contend with our Maker.

While it is true that the material of which man is made is next to nothing, the one who made us is the Creator and, thereby, able to do all things. Consequently, we should say as David said, *"I will praise You; for I am fearfully and wonderfully made: marvelous are Your works; and that my soul knows right well"* (Ps. 139:14).

Men judge the value of an item according to the material of which it is made. The worth of that which God creates pertains to Him. His hand can make something of nothing.

THE BREATH OF LIFE

The statement, *"And breathed into his nostrils the breath of life; and man became a living soul,"* pertains to man being unique in that nothing else in God's creation received the breath of God. This means that life came not as the result of man's bodily organization or as derived by evolution from any animal but as a gift directly from God.

Delitzsch said: "By an act of divine omnipotence man arose from the dust, and in the same moment in which the dust, by virtue of creative omnipotence, shaped itself into the human form, it was pervaded by the divine breath of life, and created a living being, so that we cannot say the body was earlier than the soul."[3]

The breath of life, which comes from God, pertains to the soul and spirit of man. This was done with the first man with God breathing the soul and the spirit into man, and, thereafter, it comes automatically at conception.

THE GARDEN OF EDEN

"And the LORD *God planted a garden eastward in Eden; and there He put the man whom He had formed"* (Gen. 2:8).

This garden was the garden of Eden. It was actually planted before Adam was created.

It was planted eastward in Eden, which some scholars believe was ultimately the site of the city of Babylon.

There He placed the man.

"Eastward in Eden," no doubt, meant east of Israel. Of course, at the time this was written, Israel did not exist; however, the Holy Spirit definitely knew that in time, it would exist.

MAN'S HOME

The phrase, *"And there He put the man whom He had formed,"* proclaims the place especially prepared for man.

From this we realize that God began preparing for man even before he was created. After the fall, the greatest preparation of all was undertaken in respect to redemption, which would require a price to be paid that beggars all description. Then, concerning the eternal abode, Jesus said: *"I go to prepare a place for you. And if I go and prepare a place for you, I will come again, and receive you unto Myself; that where I am, there you may be also"* (Jn. 14:2–3).

So, in all of this, we see the tender love, mercy, and compassion of God as it regards His choice creation—man. He prepared a garden for man; He prepared salvation for man; and now, He has prepared a paradise that so far outstrips the garden of Eden as to be no contest. As stated, all of this portrays the love of God.

GOOD FOR FOOD

"And out of the ground made the LORD *God to grow every tree that is pleasant to the sight, and good for food; the Tree of Life also in the midst of the garden, and the tree of knowledge of good and evil"* (Gen. 2:9).

The phrase, *"And out of the ground made the* LORD *God to grow every tree that is pleasant to the sight, and good for food,"* refers to every type of beautiful tree for adornment, every fruit tree imaginable, and even those which bear nuts.

In fact, according to the creation of day three, the entirety of the earth had these types of trees. So, these particular trees in the garden of Eden must have been of special type and were given special care by the Lord. The trees, no doubt, were more beautiful, with the fruit trees bearing fruit that was more luscious, and the trees bearing nuts falling into the same category. Without toil and without labor, everything that man needed was amply provided, and then some. The provision of God lacked nothing.

TREE OF LIFE

The phrase, *"The tree of life also in the midst of the garden,"* evidently means that it contained a type of fruit. Genesis 3:22 says as much!

Ellicott said, "The tree of life had the power of so renewing man's physical energies that his body though formed of the dust of the ground, and therefore naturally mortal, would, by its continual use, live on forever."[4]

Christ is now to us the *"Tree of Life"* (Rev. 2:7; 22:2) and the *"Bread of Life"* (Jn. 6:48, 51).

What type of fruit the Tree of Life did bear, we aren't told. There are some who suppose it may have been an apple tree, with divine properties appropriated for this particular fruit. This is derived from the Song of Solomon 2:3.

Even though man's physical body was formed out of dust, by the properties of the Tree of Life, it was meant to live forever. Death was not in the original plan. That came by sin.

It seems that men with natural bodies will come and go in the New Jerusalem and will live forever by virtue of the Tree of Life and the fruit that it will bear every month (Rev. 22:2).

This does not refer to those with glorified bodies (which will be in the coming kingdom age), who will not need such sustenance in order to live eternally. This will include all who have part in the first resurrection (Rev. 20:6).

THE TREE OF KNOWLEDGE OF GOOD AND EVIL

The phrase, *"and the tree of knowledge of good and evil,"* presents the tree of death.

One might say that the tree of death appears at the opening of the Bible, the tree of Calvary (I Pet. 2:24) in the middle of the Bible, and the Tree of Life at the end of the Bible (Rev. 2:7).

Due to the manner in which Adam and Eve were created as free moral agents, this agency had to be tested. The Tree of Knowledge of Good and Evil served as the vehicle for that testing. It was not that its fruit contained some type of poisonous property, but it was rather the act of disobedience to God in eating this fruit. God had said that they must not eat of the fruit of that tree, so their disobedience is what constituted the fall.

What is meant here by good and evil?

Taking the latter first, Adam and Eve knew nothing about evil whatsoever. At the beginning of their creation, they were in total harmony with God and knew only righteousness. So, the evil at that time was only a curiosity, but it was such curiosity that did them in.

Unfortunately, due to Adam's fall, the entirety of the human race has an expert knowledge of evil. To be sure, it's a knowledge we wish we didn't have, for it has been the bane of society and of humanity in general. However, it's the knowledge of good that stumps most people. What, in fact, is meant by the words "knowledge of good?"

THE KNOWLEDGE OF GOOD

Inasmuch as both of these principles (good and evil) are on one tree, we then know that the good addressed here carries with it a very negative connotation.

It refers to the good that men attempt to carry out, which they think earns them salvation or favor with God. Most of all, they think that it atones in some way. Because it is good— whatever *it* might be—it deceives people. Let the reader please understand that this type of good covers a wide spectrum.

It runs the gamut all the way from the unredeemed trying to earn salvation, which most do, to the Christian attempting to earn victory. Both are trying by doing good things.

In the first place, the good that man does is already polluted because it's touched by human hands, and once this is done, the good is then sullied. Irrespective, none of this earns anything with God. In other words, the good that man does will not spend in God's economy.

The Scripture plainly says the following: *"For by grace are you saved through faith; and that not of yourselves: it is the gift of God: Not of works, lest any man should boast"* (Eph. 2:8–9).

Paul further said, *"But God forbid that I should glory, save in the Cross of our Lord Jesus Christ, by whom the world is crucified unto me, and I unto the world"* (Gal. 6:14).

A man came to Jesus one day and asked Him, *"Good Master, what good thing shall I do, that I may have eternal life? And He said unto him, Why do you call Me good? there is none good but one, that is, God"* (Mat. 19:16–17).

THE ONLY WAY TO GOD

It may seem at first glance that Jesus was saying here that He personally wasn't good; however, that's not what He was saying. He was saying that the only one who is good is God. Considering that Christ is God, then He is good.

However, when it comes to man, there is no good thing that he can do that will give him eternal life, but yet, he continues to think that he can arrive at that destination in this manner.

The only way to God is through Christ Jesus and what He did at the Cross and our faith in that finished work. If we try to come any other way, we will be judged by God as a *"thief and a robber"* (Jn. 10:1). That's where the world runs aground, and regrettably, that's where the church runs aground! This particular knowledge, whether of good or evil, we don't want. We only want one kind of knowledge: *"For God, who commanded the light to shine out of darkness, has shined in our hearts, to give the light of the knowledge of the glory of God in the face of Jesus Christ"* (II Cor. 4:6).

A RIVER

"And a river went out of Eden to water the garden; and from thence it was parted, and became into four heads" (Gen. 2:10).

This could mean the river parted while in Eden, with four streams proceeding forth, or it could mean that the river flowed through the garden and parted into four streams after leaving the garden.

PISON

"The name of the first is Pison: that is it which compasseth the whole land of Havilah, where there is gold" (Gen. 2:11).

This is said to be India, with the river now called the Ganges.

PRECIOUS METAL AND PRECIOUS STONES

"And the gold of that land is good: there is bdellium and the onyx stone" (Gen. 2:12).

Gold is mentioned here and in Verse 11, which is the first mention in the Bible of this precious metal. It is mentioned last in the Bible as it refers to the main thoroughfare of the New Jerusalem, which we are told is *"pure gold"* (Rev. 21:21).

GIHON

"And the name of the second river is Gihon: the same is it that compasseth the whole land of Ethiopia" (Gen. 2:13).

This river is believed to be the Nile.

HIDDEKEL AND EUPHRATES

"And the name of the third river is Hiddekel: that is it which goes toward the east of Assyria. And the fourth river is Euphrates" (Gen. 2:14).

This proclaims the last two rivers. Hiddekel is believed to be the Tigris, with Euphrates maintaining its name even unto the present hour.

These rivers at the present time have their sources far apart. The explanation, no doubt, lies in the flood, which altered the topography of the earth. The headwaters of the first two were drastically changed, while the last two remain basically the same.

In fact, it is believed that the garden of Eden may have been located at the joining of the Tigris and Euphrates, which is the site of ancient Babylon.

We find this river, which was a literal river, starting to flow in the garden of Eden. It was soon marred by sin, which necessitated the flood, which wrecked the headwaters.

Spiritually speaking, the river appears again, not from Eden, but from the smitten rock. Paul said, *"That Rock was Christ."*

Passing onward, we find the river flowing in another channel. *"In the last day, that great day of the feast, Jesus stood and cried, saying, If any man thirst, let him come unto Me, and drink. He who believes on Me, as the Scripture has said, out of his belly* (innermost being) *shall flow rivers of living water"* (Jn. 7:37–38).

Mackintosh said, "Finally, we have the river of God presented to us in the last chapter of the book of Revelation. The Scripture says, 'And He showed me a pure river of water of life, clear as crystal, proceeding out of the throne of God and of the Lamb' (Rev. 22:1)."⁵

This is the last place in which we find the river. Its source can never again be touched; its channel can never again be interrupted. It is based now on the ground of accomplished redemption, which points to Christ and His Cross.

Here we have the throne of God, which is expressive of eternal stability. It is not God's throne in creation or in providence, but rather in redemption.

When I see *"the Lamb,"* I always know its connection with me is as a sinner. As such, *"the throne of God"* would but deter me; however, when God reveals Himself in the person of the Lamb, the heart is attracted and the conscience tranquilized.

Mackintosh said:

The blood of the Lamb cleanses the conscience from every speck and stain of sin, and sets it, in perfect freedom, in the presence of a holiness which cannot tolerate sin. In the Cross, all the claims of divine holiness were perfectly answered, so that the more I understand the latter, the more I appreciate the former. The higher our estimate of holiness, the higher will be our estimate of the work of the Cross. 'Grace reigns, through righteousness, unto eternal life, by Jesus Christ our Lord'⁶

THE MAN

"And the LORD *God took the man, and put him into the garden of Eden to dress it and to keep it"* (Gen. 2:15).

The *"*LORD *God"* is Jehovah Elohim.

The phrase, *"And the* LORD *God took the man,"* in effect, means that the Lord told him to go to the garden, which had been prepared especially for him. So, we see here that God exerts special care for His prime creation. The Lord not only created him, but, as well, He prepared for him, and now He will give him responsibility.

TO DRESS IT AND KEEP IT

The phrase, *"And put him into the garden of Eden to dress it and to keep it,"* presents his particular task for that particular time. So, in a very real sense is every man's life occupation appointed by God. "To every man his work" is the law of God's world as well as of Christ's kingdom. This thought should dignify the trivial task and, thereby, enable us so that whether we eat or drink—or whatever we do—we do all to the glory of God.

Every believer in the world has a special work designed especially for him that is intended for him to do. Unfortunately, far too many believers try to do something that God never called them to do, or else, through apathy and unbelief, they do nothing. Happy are the man and woman who find the will of God for their respective lives and then carry out that will. Such will always bring happiness, joy, fulfillment, and purpose.

Unfortunately, many Christians do not think of what they are presently doing as being of any consequence. Such thinking is wrong!

As a believer, irrespective of what we do—even if it's cooking hamburgers at a McDonald's—we should realize that God put us there, and we should do the very best service that we can do. Quite possibly, the Lord places many of His children in similar circumstances in order to be a witness at a proven time. If we're looking for the opportunity, to be sure, the opportunity will definitely present itself.

Nothing happens by chance to the child of God. All is planned, approved, and carried out by the Lord. If it's a mess up, so to speak, then the mess up is all on our part and never on God's part.

Wherever the Lord puts you, you are to look at the task before you and irrespective of how menial it may seem to be, you are then to *"dress it and to keep it."*

THE COMMAND

"And the LORD *God commanded the man, saying, Of every tree of the garden you may freely eat: But of the tree of the knowledge of good and evil, you shall not eat of it: for in the day that you eat thereof you shall surely die"* (Gen. 2:16-17).

Verse 16 begins by stating, *"And the* LORD *God commanded the man,"* which means there was only one command from God to keep. And yet, the command presented a stern warning, which, in effect, proclaims the first and only command to Adam before the fall. Probation is the law of man's moral condition now, and it began in Paradise, only the conditions there were different.

As the Creator, God had the right to issue such a command and to expect man to obey. In this we learn that man was a free moral agent. He was not a machine, but he had the power of reason and, as well, a will. In other words, he could choose to obey the Lord or disobey the Lord, which is obvious from the command given.

Also, the word *commanded* should not be taken lightly. It was a strong, powerful statement, which was meant to impress upon Adam the severity of the situation, that is, if he disobeyed!

THREE DIVINE INSTITUTIONS

In a sense, one might say that with this command, the church was formed here. If, in fact, that is the case, and it certainly seems to be, this would mean that the church was the first of the three great divine institutions formed by God.

They are:

1. The church

2. The home

3. Civil government

With the creation of Eve, the home would have been second, and civil government would have come last. This became necessary only when man's nature was corrupted. It is the business of civil government to oppose sin as Paul declares in Romans 13:4. Had Adam not sinned, civil government would not have been necessary, for man would have lived in perfect peace, rest, and security, for there would have been no robber, murderer, or thief. So, Adam would have needed only the church and the home.

So, in a sense, inasmuch as the church was the first divine institution formed, we would have to say that it is more important even than the home or civil government. It has well been said, and probably correctly, that as the church goes, so goes the home, and so goes the nation.

THE TREE OF THE KNOWLEDGE
OF GOOD AND EVIL

Verse 16 further reads, *"Saying, Of every tree of the garden you may freely eat."*

Verse 17 begins by stating, *"But of the tree of the knowledge of good and evil, you shall not eat of it,"* which constituted the command.

As stated, Adam was given only one command, and that was in a Paradise. By contrast, Jesus, as the last Adam, had to keep every commandment of the law, with His probationary period beginning in a wilderness (Mat., Chpt. 4). Jesus was in the wilderness with the wild beasts (Mk. 1:13), while Adam was in Paradise with animals that were beautiful and docile.

Many would ask the question of why God placed this tree in the garden. They reason that without the Tree of the

Knowledge of Good and Evil, there would have been no fall and, thereby, no problem.

Let the reader understand that the Tree of the Knowledge of Good and Evil was not the cause of Adam's fall. It was a failure to heed and obey the word of God, which is the cause of every single failure.

So, why would Adam do such a thing? He had no sin nature as all who followed him have. He had every tree in the garden of which he could eat of their fruit, and only one tree of which he was commanded not to eat.

TESTING

As to why he did what he did, I don't think I can answer that question; furthermore, I don't think it can be answered by any human being.

The tree had to be there, for man had to be tested. It wasn't that God had to test Adam in order that He (God) might know what Adam would do, for God already knew. It was that Adam might know!

Some, who reason that if God had given Adam a will-power that was so strong that he could amply resist, miss the point altogether. For a will to be that which is proper, at the same time, it has to be able to say yes or no. Otherwise, it's not a will.

Psychology claims that the environment is the answer. In other words, if a proper environment can be provided, this will stop all sin and sinning. Well, let me remind the reader that Adam was in a perfect environment when he sinned. So, that's not the cause or the cure!

It comes down to obedience or disobedience. We need to look at that.

THE WILL OF MAN

Almost all Christians misunderstand what the will of man actually is.

While it is true that we are free moral agents, and while it is also true that we have the power of choice, the truth is, we need to understand exactly what is being said here.

Most Christians think that once they have come to Christ, they then have the willpower to either say yes or no to whatever it is they so desire. Nothing could be further from the truth.

While the believer definitely does have the power to say yes or no, it is only in one category. That category pertains to Christ.

In other words, the Christian can say yes or no to Christ, and that's where his will begins, and that's where his will ends. To be more particular, this yes or no must pertain not only to Christ, but what Christ did at the Cross on our behalf. The essence of this is that we can say yes to what Christ has done for us at the Cross and rely totally and completely on His finished work, or we can say no.

If we say no, we then close the door to the Holy Spirit. This leaves us facing the powers of darkness with nothing but our own personal strength, i.e., willpower, which we will find every time to be totally inadequate.

No, the Christian is doomed to failure if he thinks he can face the sin business and simply say yes or no. That's not the way it works. Those who try that (and almost all have) will conclude by failing every time. You may win for awhile, but after awhile, you're going to fail.

Now, stop and think about this for a moment: If it were possible for us to defeat sin and the attacks of Satan by willpower, then Jesus would not have had to come down here and die on a Cross. He could have merely taught us how to function within our willpower, and that would have solved the problem.

However, He didn't do that, did He? The truth is, the problem of sin is so deadly that it took the Cross to defeat this monster, and even then, we have to have the help of the Holy Spirit to get this thing done. That's why Paul said, *"But if the Spirit* (Holy Spirit) *of Him* (God the Father) *who raised up Jesus from the dead dwell in you, He who raised up Christ from the dead shall also quicken your mortal bodies by His Spirit who dwells in you"* (Rom. 8:11).

This tells us that sin is so powerful that it takes the same power to overcome this thing as it did to raise Jesus from the dead, which, of course, is the power of the Holy Spirit. Understanding that, we should come to the conclusion that our personal willpower is totally inadequate.

However, most Christians little understand the victory of the Cross and try to do this thing on their own, which always results in failure.

A SIMPLE DIAGRAM

The following diagram is very simple, but perhaps it will help you to understand more fully what we are saying. The following, in extremely abbreviated form, constitutes the means by which any and every Christian can walk in victory, and by that, we mean perpetual victory:

- Focus. The focus of every believer must always be on the Lord Jesus Christ, realizing that He is the source of all things that we receive from God (Jn. 1:1-3, 14, 29; 14:6, 20; Rom. 6:1-14).

- Object of faith. The object of our faith must, as well, always rest on Jesus Christ and what He did for us at the Cross. In other words, it's who He is and what He did. The finished work of Christ must always be the pivot point in our consecration. Unfortunately, too many Christians have other things as the object of their faith, which guarantees failure (I Cor. 1:17, 18, 23; 2:2; Col. 2:10-15).

- Power source. With our focus on the Cross of Christ, which means that the finished work of Christ is now the object of our faith, our power source is now the Holy Spirit, who always works within the parameters of the finished work of Christ. This is why the object of our faith is so very, very important (Rom. 8:1-11; Eph. 2:13-18).

- Results. Having the Cross as our focus and the finished work as the object of our faith, which guarantees the Holy Spirit being the power source, then we cannot fail. It is victory to victory, or we should say, faith to faith (Rom. 6:14; I Cor. 2:2; Col. 2:14-15).

ERRONEOUS DIRECTION

Now, let's use the same formula, but yet, turn it around. Regrettably, this is the place and position of most modern Christians.

I am going to give the same points but position it the way it is being addressed by most modern Christians. Read them carefully:

- Focus. Not understanding the victory of the Cross as it regards sanctification, most modern Christians focus on works.

- Object of faith. Focusing on works, the object of our faith becomes our performance, which is always inadequate because the Holy Spirit will not function in this capacity.

- Power source. By focusing on works and trusting in our performance, the power source now is self.

- Results. By focusing on works, with the object of our faith being our personal performance and the power source now being self, the results are predictable—failure. As stated, this latter diagram is the place and position of most modern Christians. In other words, they simply don't know how to live for God.

THE CROSS

The reason for the failure is because of not knowing and understanding the Message of the Cross. Paul said, *"For the preaching of the Cross is to them who perish foolishness; but unto us who are saved it is the power of God"* (I Cor. 1:18).

The Greek word here translated "preaching" is *logos.* It should have been translated "word" or "message." It would then have read: "For the message of the Cross is to them ..."

Regrettably and sadly, very few Christians know the Message of the Cross. They don't know it simply because it's not being preached and taught behind their pulpits. Considering that *"faith comes by hearing, and hearing by the Word of God,"* if the Word of God is not taught in this capacity, then the person can have no faith in that which he does not know (Rom. 10:17).

For one to properly understand the Word of God, one must understand the word of the Cross. In fact, the story of the Bible is the story of the Cross simply because it's the story of man's redemption. So, to try and understand the Bible apart from the Cross simply will not work. That's why Paul also said, *"For I determined not to know anything among you, save Jesus Christ, and Him crucified"* (I Cor. 2:2).

FAITH

I am sure that every believer knows and understands that faith is the currency, so to speak, that spends in God's economy. In fact, it's the only currency that He will accept, but let the reader understand the following: When Paul spoke of faith, which he did constantly in one way or the other, without exception, he was always speaking of faith in Christ and what Christ did at the Cross.

In fact, he even referred to this great Christian experience as "the *faith*" (Gal. 2:20).

However, if the faith of which we speak is not faith in Christ and Him crucified, then it's faith that God will not recognize. Regrettably, as it pertains to the Lord, most Christians presently have faith in about everything except the Cross. They claim to have faith in the Word, but they fail to understand that if it's not faith in the Cross, then it's not faith in the Word. The two—faith and the Word—are synonymous.

THE WORD BECAME FLESH

Listen to this: John said, *"In the beginning was the Word, and the Word was with God, and the Word was God"* (Jn. 1:1).

This tells us that Jesus was the living Word.

He then said, *"And the Word was made flesh, and dwelt among us"* (Jn. 1:14).

The Lord became flesh in order to be the last Adam and, thereby, to go to the Cross.

When John introduced Christ, he then said, *"Behold the Lamb of God, which takes away the sin of the world"* (Jn. 1:29).

We now know why the Word became flesh. It was that He might go to the Cross, which was demanded, that is, if man was to be redeemed. So, if we claim to understand the Word or to have our faith based on the Word, which is certainly correct, that is, if we know what we're talking about, then we must understand that the Cross must ever be the object of our faith. Then the Word will begin to come into sharp focus.

Now, let me make this statement; I know it's controversial, but it needs to be said: If the believer doesn't properly understand the Message of the Cross, then in some way, everything he thinks he understands about the Word of God will be more or less perverted.

SPIRITUAL DEATH

Verse 17 further reads, *"For in the day that you eat thereof you shall surely die,"* refers to spiritual death, which is separation from God. In other words, at the moment that Adam partook of that particular fruit, whatever it was, he died, i.e., was separated from God. Regrettably and sadly, spiritual death brought on physical death. Unless one turns to Christ, the concluding result will be *"the second death,"* which is the lake of fire, forever and forever (Rev. 20:14).

We know, as we shall see, that Adam had an amazing intelligence. In fact, I think that no man since has had the intelligence level of Adam, at least that which he had before the fall. But yet,

I'm not sure if he fully understood what the word *die* actually meant. Considering that he was created to live forever by virtue of the Tree of Life, death, as it is presently, was not in his thinking or understanding.

Even though the Bible doesn't exactly say, I do believe that God explained to him what all of this meant, even as he gave him the command not to eat of the fruit of the Tree of the Knowledge of Good and Evil. Knowing the detailed account of the creation and the meticulous way in which God does things, I must believe that He meticulously explained all of this to our first parent. Regrettably, as we shall see, Adam chose to disobey.

A COMPANION

"And the LORD *God said, It is not good that the man should be alone; I will make him an help meet for him"* (Gen. 2:18).

As we shall see, these statements are not meant to imply that the creation of woman was an afterthought. There is no plan of God that is incomplete!

The phrase, *"And the* LORD *God said, It is not good that the man should be alone,"* was not an idea that suddenly presented itself to the Lord. God is omnipotent (all-powerful) and omniscient (all-knowing), meaning that there are no surprises with God or any situation that presents itself of which He doesn't have full knowledge. From the time that the Godhead had made the decision to create man, whenever that may have been in eternity past, the creation of woman was planned as well.

HELPMATE

The phrase, *"I will make him an help meet for him,"* proclaims the fact that the Lord did exactly that. He made a helpmate for Adam and made it possible for all men who would follow thereafter to have the same. What a blessing!

All that Adam's nature demanded for its completion—physically, intellectually, and socially—was to be included in this one who was soon to stand by his side. Thus, in man's need, and woman's power to satisfy that need, is laid the foundation for the divine institution of marriage, which was afterwards prescribed not for the first pair alone, but for all their posterity. I remind the reader that it was Adam and Eve, not Adam and Steve.

BROUGHT THEM UNTO ADAM

"And out of the ground the LORD *God formed every beast of the field, and every fowl of the air; and brought them unto Adam to see what he would call them: and whatsoever Adam called every living creature, that was the name thereof"* (Gen. 2:19).

Out of dust, the Lord God formed every beast of the field and every fowl of the air. Adam gave names to all of these creatures. In the name he gave to each creature, we find the entirety of the characteristics of that particular animal or fowl. This proves that this man was brilliant beyond compare.

The phrase, *"And out of the ground the* LORD *God formed every beast of the field, and every fowl of the air; and brought them unto Adam,"* pertains to specimens.

We must understand that this chapter is not intended to be a chronology of creation. The narrative runs according to what is being done at the moment.

LIVING CREATURES

The phrase, *"To see what he would call them: and whatsoever Adam called every living creature, that was the name thereof,"* presents two things:

1. As we have already stated, the name that Adam gave to each one of these creatures presents the characteristics of that particular animal or fowl. Let the reader understand that the name hasn't changed from then until now.

2. Before the fall, Adam walked with God every day in the cool of the day, which gave him an education of unparallel proportions (Gen. 3:8-9). This proclaims to us the fact that Adam was of such intelligence as to defy all description. What type of intelligence does it take for one to know all the characteristics of these creatures!

So, I think it should be overly obvious that we aren't speaking here of a dolt or an animal-crawling primate, as suggested by some.

To do all of this, Adam had to have a distinct knowledge of speech, the meaning of all words, and the capacity for attaching words to ideas.

Why not? Adam had the greatest teacher that man has ever had—the LORD God.

NAMES

"And Adam gave names to all cattle, and to the fowl of the air, and to every beast of the field; but for Adam there was not found a help meet for him" (Gen. 2:20).

Verse 20 proclaims the amazing degree of intelligence possessed by earth's first man. When we understand that these names incorporate every characteristic of each particular creature, and that these names come down to us unto this very hour, then we are forced to recognize the amazing intelligence possessed by Adam.

If man had not fallen, the world would have been a far different place, which is actually a gross understatement. In fact, there's really no way that we can even remotely comprehend what would have been. We get some idea from the prophets as they spoke of the coming kingdom age; however, even then, there will still be sin in the world, despite the fact that Jesus will be personally ruling from Jerusalem. But yet, at that particular time, the world will come close to that which God originally intended.

SIN

Man has repeatedly attempted to rebuild this Paradise himself. He has done so with socialism, communism, dictatorships, etc. That which points in the right direction is biblical democracy, one might say. However, let it quickly be understood that a **true** democracy cannot be built and cannot be brought into being without the Bible being its foundation. America spent a trillion dollars and wasted over 4,000 lives in the quagmire of Iraq, trying to build a democratic nation without addressing the religion of Islam. It cannot be done. As one man said, "Democracy and Islam aren't even on the same planet."

Now, when I say that a democracy must be built upon the Bible, this is not an advocating of a state church. It is far from such! The separation of church and state is biblical, but that doesn't mean the separation of God and state as is being carried on in America presently. Unless it's changed, it will be the ruin of this nation. It is still, "**In God we trust.**"

Man's problem is that he tries to do it without the Tree of Life, which, incidentally, is the Lord Jesus Christ. Such simply cannot be done without Christ. The hearts of men are far too wicked, and, incidentally, they are hearts that can only be changed by Christ. Even then, He had to pay a terrible price by the giving of Himself in sacrifice on the Cross in order that this terrible problem of sin might be properly addressed. Regrettably, the world refuses to understand the terrible malady of sin, although it fills the earth with hatred, murder, and mayhem.

THE CROSS OF CHRIST

Even the church, I think, doesn't fully realize the terrible horror of sin, and I'll tell you why I say that: If the church fully understood the malady of sin as they should, they wouldn't keep advocating foolish things as its cure rather than the Cross. The Cross of Christ is the only answer to sin. That refers to the sinner being saved or the Christian attempting to walk holy before the Lord. If we look to anything else, our looking is in vain! There is no help in any other direction.

This is why Paul said, *"We preach Christ crucified"* (I Cor. 1:23). He didn't say merely, *"We preach Christ,"* but rather, *"We preach Christ crucified."* The problem with the church is that it preaches Christ but in many and varied ways other than the Cross. Many preach Him as the great example; others preach Him as the healer; and others preach Him as the great prosperity-giver. In fact, the list is almost endless. However, unless Christ is preached as the Saviour, and the Saviour by virtue of what He did at the Cross, lives will never be changed. That's why Paul said what he did.

PSYCHOLOGY

Unfortunately, much of the modern church world, in fact, virtually all, has opted for the psychological way.

Let the reader understand first of all that the psychological way and the way of the Cross are diametrically opposed to each other. They are so diametrically different and originating from such totally different sources that there is no way the two can be wedded.

As for preachers who claim that the two can be melded, it shows either a terrible ignorance of the Cross of Christ, or else, gross unbelief.

The Lord began to open up to me the revelation of the Cross in 1997. That revelation continues unto this hour. At that time, I felt that the foray of the church into humanistic psychology was, for the most part, caused by ignorance of the Word of God. While that certainly is the case with some, after several years now of observing the church scene with much more knowledgeable eyes, I regrettably must come to the conclusion that the real reason the Cross has been abandoned is because of rank unbelief. To be sure, that is the most dangerous position of all. Ignorance can be corrected, but it is far harder to correct unbelief.

In fact, for unbelief to be corrected, one has to completely and totally renounce the erroneous way that one is traveling, which is very difficult for most to do.

PERSONAL

The reason that virtually all of the church world denounces my person is because of this very thing that we are presently addressing—the Cross. They may claim other things constitute the reason, but the other things are actually only excuses. The real reason has always been, and is presently, our stand regarding the Lord Jesus Christ and the Cross upon which He died. We claim the Cross is the answer and, in fact, the only answer for hurting humanity. They claim, whomever they might be, that other things are the answer, hence, the juxtaposition.

Admittedly, in 1988, I did not know and understand the Cross as it regarded the sanctification of the saint. To be sure, I understood the Cross as it regarded the initial salvation experience, and I preached it about as strongly as anyone in the world. As a result, the Lord gave us literally hundreds of thousands of souls, for which we give Him all of the praise and all of the glory.

However, not knowing and understanding the Cross as it regards our everyday walk before God, in fact, I was actually reliving Chapter 7 of Romans.

ROMANS, CHAPTER SEVEN

This chapter catalogs Paul's experience after he was saved and baptized with the Holy Spirit and actually called to be an apostle. However, at that time he did not know the victory of the Cross and, as a result, was attempting to live for Christ by his own strength, etc. Despite trying so hard, he failed, and the following are his exact words: *"For that which I do I allow* (understand) *not: for what I would, that do I not; but what I hate, that do I"* (Rom. 7:15).

Then he said, *"For I know that in me (that is, in my flesh,) dwells no good thing: for to will is present with me; but how to perform that which is good I find not"* (Rom. 7:18).

He plainly tells us here that he was trying to live for God by the virtue of willpower but found to his dismay that the will alone wasn't enough.

That's where I was, and that's where millions of Christians are presently. They're trying with all of their strength to live as they ought to live but failing miserably. The sad fact is that the harder they struggle, the worse the situation actually becomes. They are left very, very confused. So, what are such Christians doing?

Strangely enough, many of these particular Christians are some of the hardest workers for the Lord in the world. In fact, some of them are extremely consecrated to the Lord.

THE VICTORY OF THE CROSS

Now, an unbelieving church may not agree with that, claiming that such cannot be, but the truth is, the ones doing the criticizing are in worse shape, spiritually speaking, than the ones toward whom they are leveling the criticism.

It doesn't matter what a believer does or how hard he tries, if he doesn't know and understand the victory of the Cross, he will fall. Understanding the victory of the Cross simply means that he is to know that everything comes to him from God by and through what Jesus did at the Cross, and that his faith must ever be in the finished work of Christ (Rom. 6:3–5, 11, 14). With this done, and continuing to be done even on a daily basis (Lk. 9:23), the Holy Spirit will then work mightily on behalf of the believer, which will guarantee victory on a perpetual basis (Rom. 8:1–2, 11).

However, if the Christian doesn't know this and, thereby, seeks to live for God by other means and ways, he is doomed to failure, irrespective of whom he might be.

FAILURE

As stated, in 1988, I did not know this, and despite trying so very, very hard, I failed. I might quickly add that such failure is inevitable if the believer doesn't understand the Cross.

Despite the shame, humiliation, pain, and suffering, if the believer continues in his lack of understanding, the failure will continue, as well, no matter how hard he tries otherwise. Unfortunately, pain and suffering are not the cure that will give victory over the attacks by the powers of darkness.

So, my enemies, of whom I seemed to have had many, took full advantage of that. However, the real reason was that I was preaching the Cross. Admittedly, I was only preaching it as it regarded the salvation of sinners, but at the same time, I was still loudly saying on a worldwide basis that the psychological way was wrong. That didn't set very well with the leaders of particular denominations, considering that they had embraced the psychological way in totality. So, when an opportunity presented itself for them to exact their pound of flesh, they took full advantage. However, again, the reason wasn't what it seemed to be to the world, but rather what I preached, and I speak of the Cross.

THE OFFENSE OF THE CROSS

Paul said, *"And I, brethren, if I yet preach circumcision, why do I yet suffer persecution? then is the offense of the Cross ceased"* (Gal. 5:11).

The Holy Spirit through the apostle plainly tells us here that the Cross of Christ is an offense, not only to the world, but to many in the church. In other words, if one preaches the Cross, lives the Cross, and places his faith and confidence totally and completely in what Christ did at the Cross, that will be an offense to many so-called Christians.

Why?

One of the reasons this happens is that there is something in all believers that desires to live this life for Christ by our own strength and ability. It is a carry over from the fall. As a result, it's very hard for us to completely deny ourselves and, thereby, totally trust Christ (Lk. 9:23). So, the tendency is always there as it regards dependence on the flesh.

Then again, religious man doesn't mind working unceasingly and untiringly, depriving himself and his family, if he thinks that will grant him favor from God, simply because such effort ministers to his own self importance. Look what I have done! However, it is effort that God cannot accept because it's built on the wrong foundation.

ORGANIZED RELIGION

Organized religion always builds up a dependence on the organization. In other words, little by little it pulls preachers into a dependence on what that organization can do for them, which even carries over to their everyday life and living. In fact, all believers who belong to that particular denomination are, much of the time, made to believe that the mere association with that organization brings some type of spirituality. This, of course, is done a little bit at a time.

So, trust, faith, and dependence on Christ and what He has done for us at the Cross are eroded a little at a time and are replaced by faith in the denomination. It is so subtle that the person hardly knows that it's happening.

When the believer begins to depend totally and completely on the Cross of Christ, and I speak of what Jesus did there for us, he will run headlong into *"the flesh"* of organized religion. This is what Paul was talking about as it regarded the offense of the Cross.

At the first part of Galatians 5:11, Paul mentioned the preaching of circumcision. In effect, he was saying that if he continued to preach circumcision (speaking of a dependence on the law) and joined that to Christ, then the offense of the Cross would cease. However, when he told the church that circumcision and adherence to the law availed them nothing at all, but rather that which Jesus did at the Cross, that struck a nerve. To be sure, that nerve is still in view presently in many and varied ways.

THE CROSS

So, if the believer charts a course that takes him strictly to the Cross and total dependence on the Cross, it's going to rub a lot of fur the wrong way. To trust completely in Christ and what Christ did for us at the Cross, at the same time, means to throw over everything else—all the religious props, denominational attachments, personal strength and ability, everything.

No, this doesn't mean that it's wrong to belong to a denomination or a church. It just means that it's wrong to put faith and confidence in these things, considering that they are merely man-made and man-devised efforts and institutions. However, the point I wish to make is this: Once we begin to trust exclusively in Christ and what Christ has done for us at the Cross, of necessity this cuts off everything else.

This is actually what Paul was meaning when he said, *"I would* (wish) *they were even cut off which trouble you"* (Gal. 5:12).

In other words, there were Judaizers who were trying to get the Galatians to embrace the law along with Christ, and Paul, in essence, was saying that these people, plus their influence, had to be cut off from those who had embraced the Cross.

FELLOWSHIP

Until the Lord showed me this, it grieved me.

Let me explain: I want and desire fellowship with other brothers and sisters in the Lord. Being shunned, ostracized, and rejected is not exactly very pleasant. So, I sought the Lord earnestly about the matter.

Ultimately, He showed me that it was the Cross that drew the line. In other words, there was no way that fellowship would be forthcoming with those who had rejected the Cross. Fellowship could only be with those who had accepted the Cross. To be sure, it's not a separation that one has to enforce. The Cross itself will force the separation.

So, this means that almost all (I speak of present times) who associate themselves with denominations will little respond favorably to those who place their trust completely in the Cross. Am I saying that one cannot belong to a denomination and, at the same time, place one's faith totally and completely in Christ and what Christ has done at the Cross?

I'm not saying that at all; however, I am saying that the tendency of denominations, even as we've already stated, is to foster dependence on the denomination instead of Christ and Him crucified. As one might say, it's the nature of the beast.

Then there are those who look to the flesh, in other words, their own ability and strength. They reject the Cross in favor of commandments. There can be no fellowship in that capacity either!

So, the Lord showed me that it was not so much me they were rejecting but, in effect, the Cross.

Are they saved? Some are, and some aren't!

REJECTING THE CROSS

One thing is certain: For all who reject the Cross, even though they are truly saved, there will be no spiritual growth, and failure and defeat in some way will ever be the lot of their spiritual lives. It's impossible for it to be otherwise. The Holy Spirit through Paul plainly stated, *"I do not frustrate the grace of God: for if righteousness come by the law, then Christ is dead in vain"* (Gal. 2:21).

In other words, if we can walk in righteousness, and I speak of the righteousness that comes exclusively from the Lord, by any method other than trusting in Christ and what He did at the Cross, then Jesus didn't need to come down here and die on a Cross. So, by the very fact that He had to die on a Cross, it plainly tells us that this is the way, and there is no other. Righteousness cannot come by the law, by our own efforts, our own abilities, or by anything that man may devise. It can only come by and through what Christ did for us at the Cross and our faith in that finished work, which then guarantees the help of the Holy Spirit.

HELPMATE

The phrase, *"But for Adam there was not found an help meet for him,"* was meant to show the first man that the animal kingdom, as beautiful and helpful as some of them were, would be of no help to Adam, at least the help he needed.

To be sure, the Lord already knew all of this, but He wanted Adam to know this as well. Ellicott said, "But while he could tame many, and make them share his dwelling, he found among them (the animals) no counterpart of himself, capable of answering his thoughts and of holding with him rational discourse."[7]

The Lord knew all the time what He would do, for, in fact, it had been planned from before the foundation of the world (I Pet. 1:18–20).

I think one can say without any fear of contradiction that the Lord always creates a desire in our hearts for something that He proposes to give, although we may understand little about it to begin with.

Adam had no way of knowing what the Lord would do, but he did know that there was a deep longing within his heart for companionship—but yet, a type of companionship that would be completely compatible with himself but would not be exactly the same as himself. That's the reason he inspected the animal kingdom very closely.

EXTREMELY IMPORTANT

Other than his personal relationship with the Lord, there is nothing more important than a proper helpmate for a man. In fact, he can never really know all that the helpmate can be until he fully knows the Lord as he should.

I thank God every day of my life that He was gracious enough to give me Frances. Truly, she has filled this role and continues to fill this role to its utmost. In other words, as far as I'm concerned, it would not be possible for the Lord to have given me anything better.

When the Lord said *"helpmate,"* He meant exactly that. A woman has intuition that a man just doesn't have. She has greater sensitivity to things than the man has and, thereby, is able to discern, I think, to a greater extent.

In view of this, the Holy Spirit through Paul said, *"Wives, submit yourselves unto your own husbands, as unto the Lord"* (Eph. 5:22).

This means that the husband is to act and conduct himself as the Lord; consequently, it would not be hard for any woman to submit herself to a man of that particular character and kindness.

He then said, *"Husbands, love your wives, even as Christ also loved the church, and gave Himself for it"* (Eph. 5:25).

Christ loved the church enough to die for it. The husband is to love his wife accordingly.

AN IDEAL MARRIAGE

One of the great problems in marriage, and perhaps the greatest problem, is for the husband or wife, or both, to demand of their partner what only Christ can provide. I am persuaded that this is the cause of most marriage problems, even with Christians.

The human being can only be properly satisfied and fulfilled in Christ, but if the husband tries to make the wife meet this spiritual need or vice versa, there will be burnout. Regrettably, that is the problem with many, if not most.

Addressing Christians: One cannot really know Christ fully unless one knows and understands the Cross.

Otherwise, he is serving and trusting *"another Jesus"* (II Cor. 11:4), which means that Christ cannot truly and properly be to that person what He wants to be because his faith is misplaced.

Let's say it in a stronger way: No believer can know Christ exactly as he should unless he knows Him in relationship to the Cross. Only there can he find more abundant life (Jn. 10:10).

In truth, every single Christian in the world has more abundant life. One cannot be saved without having this particular life; however, most Christians never enjoy this life because they do not understand the Cross (Col. 2:14–15). Then, not really enjoying this life because they don't understand the Cross, they look to their mates to meet the needs in their hearts, which no human being can possibly do.

DEEP SLEEP

"And the LORD *God caused a deep sleep to fall upon Adam, and he slept: and He took one of his ribs, and closed up the flesh instead thereof"* (Gen. 2:21).

This verse records the first anesthesia. The word *rib* here actually means "side." This means the woman is not merely of a rib, but actually, of one side of man.

The phrase, *"And the* LORD *God caused a deep sleep to fall upon Adam, and he slept,"* records, as stated, the first anesthesia.

Quite obviously, the Lord explained all of this to Adam after it was done. To be sure, He, no doubt, explained every facet of His creation to the first man exactly as it is recorded here.

Even though this information, even word for word, was passed down from generation to generation, it was not until Moses, some 2,500 years after Adam, that a complete record was made in that which we now know as the book of Genesis.

Incidentally, in the Hebrew, the term *"*LORD *God"* is actually *"Yahweh God."*

THE RIB

The phrase, *"And He took one of his ribs, and closed up the flesh instead thereof,"* indicates in the Hebrew far more than a rib. It speaks of the rib with the accompanying flesh, which included the blood, the nerves, etc. This means that woman is one side of man; and though he may have several sides to his nature and character, yet without woman, one integral portion of him is wanting.

In a sense, in this procedure Adam was a figure of Him who was to come. Out of the side of Christ, the last Adam and the second man, His spouse—the church—was formed when He slept the deep sleep of death upon the Cross. In this, His side was opened, and there came out blood and water. Blood was to purchase His church, and water was to purify it to Himself (I Jn. 5:6).

BUILT A WOMAN!

"And the rib, which the LORD God had taken from man, made He a woman, and brought her unto the man" (Gen. 2:22).

The word *brought* insinuates a formal presentation, i.e., a wedding. God was the best man, so to speak!

The phrase, *"And the rib, which the LORD God had taken from man, made He a woman,"* in the Hebrew actually says, *"built He a woman."*

Horton says, "When God created the man, the word 'form' was used, which is the same word used of a potter forming a clay jar. But the word 'build' here seems to mean God paid even more attention to the creation of the woman."[8]

THE WEDDING

When Adam awakened from his deep sleep, the Lord as the attending physician was standing over him. He had placed Eve, for that's what her name would be, a distance away, perhaps hidden from view.

Then, possibly, without further explanation, but with Adam knowing that something wonderful had transpired, He presented the woman unto the man. This was the first marriage.

All of this implies the solemn bestowment of her in the bonds of the marriage covenant, which is hence called the covenant of God (Prov. 2:17), indicating that God is the author of this sacred institution.

As God was present at this wedding, He desires to be present at all weddings. The reason that over half of the marriages in this nation conclude in divorce is because God is not present at the wedding and is, therefore, little present, if at all, in the union.

If the young man and young lady will earnestly seek the Lord regarding their choice for a mate (earnestly desiring His will), to be sure, the Lord will answer this all-important prayer. Then, after marriage, if Christ is one's Lord, such a marriage will be blessed and, therefore, fruitful. Sadly, most marriages aren't in the will of God, so they little hold together.

BONE OF MY BONES, AND FLESH OF MY FLESH

"And Adam said, This is now bone of my bones, and flesh of my flesh: she shall be called woman, because she was taken out of man" (Gen. 2:23).

The phrase, *"And Adam said, This is now bone of my bones, and flesh of my flesh,"* refers to the fact that this one is proper. None of the animal kingdom would suffice simply because they were different.

However, this beautiful woman standing before Adam was bone of his bones and flesh of his flesh. He was meaning that Eve was man's counterpart, not merely in feeling and sense (his flesh), but in his solid qualities.

In several of the Semitic dialects, *bone* is used for *self*. So, in essence, he was saying, "This is now self of my self, and flesh of my flesh."

Martin Luther said concerning this moment, "The little word 'now' is very meaningful. It expresses the love of Adam, who longed for communion with a woman so full of affection and holiness. Today the bridegroom still longs for his bride, but his love is no longer pure because of sin. Adam's love for Eve was most pure, cordial, and pleasing to God."

WOMAN

The phrase, *"She shall be called woman, because she was taken out of man,"* presents a beautiful description of marriage. Everything that the man has, the woman has also. Both are of the same mind and good will toward each other so that the man differs in no way from the woman except by the dissimilarity of gender.

As someone has beautifully said, "God did not take the woman out of man's feet to be stepped on as an inferior, or out of his head to be put on a pedestal as a superior, but from his side, close to his heart as an equal."

She was to take her share of responsibility and to love him and be loved by him.

HIS WIFE

"Therefore shall a man leave his father and his mother, and shall cleave unto his wife: and they shall be one flesh" (Gen. 2:24).

This passage must be viewed as an inspired declaration of the law of marriage.

As it regards habitation, it is placed in the heart of a young man and a young woman to leave his or her parents and cleave unto a wife or husband.

"One flesh" points to a unity of persons, and not simply to a conjunction of bodies, a community of interests, or even a reciprocity of affections.

The phrase, *"Therefore shall a man leave his father and his mother, and shall cleave unto his wife,"* proclaims the plan and sanction of God regarding marriage. Let it be unequivocally understood that this in no way places a seal of approval upon same-sex marriages, which, in effect, are an abomination in the eyes of God. Homosexuality is a grievous sin and cannot be condoned under any circumstances. As stated, it is abominable in God's eyes.

In fact, it is so bad that the word translated *dogs* in Revelation 22:15 refers to homosexuals. The passage says, *"For without are dogs, and sorcerers, and whoremongers, and murderers, and idolaters, and whosoever loves and makes a lie."*

HOMOSEXUALITY

Concerning the sin of homosexuality, Paul said, *"For this cause God gave them up unto vile affections: for even their women did change the natural use into that which is against nature: And likewise also the men, leaving the natural use of the woman, burned in their lust one toward another; men with men working that which is unseemly, and receiving in themselves that recompense of their error which was meet"* (Rom. 1:26–27).

Whenever legislators legalize same-sex marriages, they are, in effect, blaspheming God. They are making a mockery out of creation, which will ultimately bring upon their heads the judgment of God. Making sin legal doesn't make it right; it only exacerbates the problem.

The hope for the homosexual, and any other sinner for that matter, in fact, for the entirety of the human race, is to come to Christ. He will deliver such a person from the terrible bondages of darkness, cleanse them, and set them free. It can only be done, however, in Christ.

Coming back to the original thought of the text, unless God unites the man and the woman, there is no real marriage but only an unhallowed connection, legitimized by man's laws, but not sanctioned by God's.

ONE FLESH

The phrase, *"And they shall be one flesh,"* pertains to one in unity and essence.

In effect, this phrase also explains the Trinity. While there are three persons in the Godhead—God the Father, God the Son, and God the Holy Spirit—they are one in unity and essence.

The *"one flesh"* is at least one of the reasons that premarital sex or extramarital activity is so wrong. Sex is to never be looked at as merely a physical pleasure. While it is that, it definitely is not merely that. It is the joining together physically of what has already been joined together spiritually. In that sense, if it is between a husband and wife who truly love each other and who truly love God, it is a holy thing.

In a broad sense, the sex act between a loving husband and wife, as stated, who truly love the Lord, is typical of one's union with Christ. As marriage is not merely a psychological or philosophical union, but something far deeper, likewise, one's union with Christ is actually likened by the Holy Spirit as marriage.

Paul said concerning this very thing, *"Wherefore, my brethren, you also are become dead to the law by the body of Christ; that you should be married to another, even to Him who is raised from the dead, that we should bring forth fruit unto God"* (Rom. 7:4).

As well, in a sense, believers are referred to by John as *"the bride, the Lamb's wife"* (Rev. 21:9).

While the union of husband and wife is one flesh, the union of Christ and the believer is, in essence, one spirit.

NAKED

"And they were both naked, the man and his wife, and were not ashamed" (Gen. 2:25).

The phrase, *"And they were both naked, the man and his wife,"* refers to clothing as we think of such presently.

Concerning God, the Scripture says, *"Who only has immortality, dwelling in the light which no man can approach unto"* (I Tim. 6:16).

This passage tells us that God is enswathed in light. Inasmuch as Adam and Eve are made in the image of God and in His likeness, it stands to reason that their original covering was the same as that of God's, which was light. In fact, this will probably be the covering of the glorified body at the first resurrection of life.

Sadly, the covering of light was lost at the fall.

ASHAMED

The phrase, *"And were not ashamed,"* is said simply because there was nothing about which to be ashamed.

When we stand one day in the celestial Eden, where they neither marry nor are given in marriage, garments of such incomparable splendor will be ours. In the meantime, let us say with Isaiah, *"I will greatly rejoice in the LORD, My soul shall be joyful in My God; for He has clothed Me with the garments of salvation, He has covered Me with the robe of righteousness, as a bridegroom decks himself with ornaments, and as a bride adorns herself with her jewels"* (Isa. 61:10).

———•◆•———

There is a name from heaven given,
God's matchless love its accents tell;
It tells of one who calls us 'brethren,'
And this His name Emmanuel!

The Lord, by angels worshipped yonder,
Has stooped to earth with men to dwell,
Incarnate God, and man forever,
Our own beloved Emmanuel.

Another name there is so precious,
It moves the heart with deepest love:
It is the blessed name of Jesus,
The name of all other names above.

It tells me that He is my Saviour,
How on the Cross His life He gave.
I love the precious name of Jesus,
For I am one He came to save!

Though dear to us the name of Jesus,
The name of Christ is also dear!
It tells of Him who dwells within us,
To cleanse our hearts and cast out fear.

It tells me of the Spirit's fullness.
It brings the pow'r of Pentecost.
O blessed Christ, come in Your fullness,
And fill me with the Holy Ghost!

These names shall live and live forever,
Eternal hope and peace they bring;
My heart is stirred whenever I hear them,
My blessed Lord, of You I sing!

How great You are, You King of Glory!
Lo, at Your feet I humbly fall,
Oh, make my heart Your holy kingdom,
That I may crown You Lord of all!

the fall of man

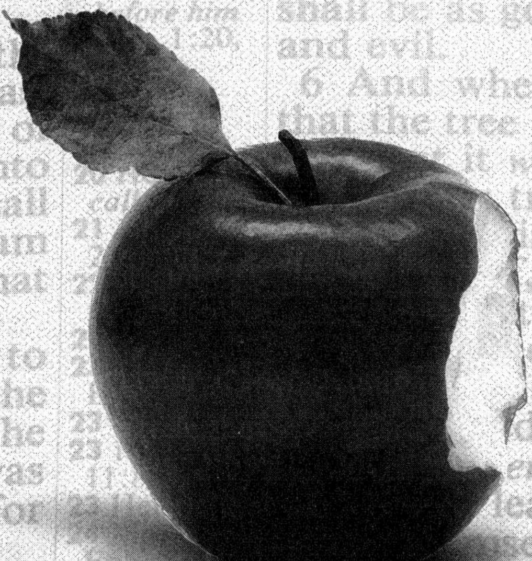

CHAPTER 3

THE TEMPTATION AND THE FALL

THE TEMPTATION AND THE FALL

"NOW THE SERPENT WAS more subtle than any beast of the field which the LORD God had made. And he said unto the woman, Yes, has God said, You shall not eat of every tree of the garden?" (Gen. 3:1).

THE SERPENT

Verse 1 draws attention to the animal that Satan used to carry out his perfidious intentions.

Due to the fact that this was before the fall and that everything God had created was good, we know that the word *subtle* used here is not negative, but rather positive. It describes qualities that, within themselves, were good, such as quickness of sight, swiftness of motion, activity of the self-preserving instinct, and seemingly intelligent adaptation to its surroundings.

As well, there is every evidence that the serpent moved upright at that time, having been consigned to its belly only after the fall as a part of the curse leveled upon it. Some argue that this is unlikely due to the skeletal make-up of the serpent; however, this could very well have changed at the fall, which it no doubt did.

SATAN

Satan is not mentioned here, but it is obvious that he is the one using the serpent as a tool.

Of course, the question must be asked if Satan was there personally or, in fact, was using a demon spirit. Actually, it seems as if he was using an evil spirit.

Satan is a fallen angel and as such, he cannot literally inhabit the physical body of anyone or anything; however, demon spirits definitely can function in this capacity and commonly do.

So, the manner of this temptation probably was that Satan was using a demon spirit to function through this animal, which evidently gave permission in some way for its body and faculties to be used. I don't think an evil spirit could have entered the body of this serpent otherwise. As well, it seems from all of this that the serpent, as well, had a limited power of choice, which means that he had a limited intelligence. If he could speak, and every evidence is that he could, then he must have had limited intelligence.

If, in fact, the serpent was an unwitting tool in the hand of Satan, then I think that the Lord would not have placed a curse upon this animal, using the words, *"Because you have done this, you are cursed"* (Gen. 3:14).

We wonder why Satan and demon spirits were even allowed in the garden or, in fact, on the earth at all.

There seems to be two reasons, which have to do with cause and effect:

1. The reason God allowed Lucifer to continue in a state of freedom after his rebellion has to come under the term *"the mystery of God"* (Rev. 10:7). This evidently took place before the world was brought back to a habitable state and before Adam and Eve were created. We do not know why the Lord allowed this, and, as well, He hasn't seen fit to reveal His reasons.

2. We do know that God uses Satan constantly. Of course, Satan's effort is to steal, kill, and destroy, but naturally, God always has something else in mind (Jn. 10:10).

As an example, man had to be tested, and even though there were, no doubt, other ways and means that God could have used, He carried out the testing by allowing Satan certain latitude in the garden. As we all know, this testing didn't turn out too well, resulting in the fall.

Our knowledge is very, very limited in all of this for the simple reason that the story of the Bible is not the story of the fall of Lucifer, but rather the story of the creation, the fall, and the redemption of mankind. Even though the Evil One plays heavily into all of this, as would be overly obvious, he is, in fact, secondary.

The principal player in the entirety of the Bible is the Lord Jesus Christ; the principal purpose is redemption; the principal object of this redemption, of course, is man, who is God's greatest creation; and the principal means by which redemption is carried out is the Cross.

DISPENSATIONS

One cannot properly understand the Bible unless one understands dispensations. The very word refers to a period of time, whether short or long.

INNOCENCE

The period of time from the creation of Adam and Eve to the fall is called the dispensation of innocence. There is no way to know exactly how long this period lasted. Some claim that it lasted only a day or so, with others claiming that it lasted a much longer period of time. It is my contention that the dispensation of innocence lasted for 40 days.

I say that because we find that the number 40 is God's number of probation in the Bible. Moses fasted 40 days and 40 nights before he began his ministry. Israel lingered 40 years in the wilderness. So, quite possibly, Adam and Eve existed in innocence for 40 days before the fall, but again, that is only speculation.

THE DISPENSATION OF CONSCIENCE

After the fall, man entered into the age or dispensation of conscience. This lasted for approximately 1,600 years, or up to the time of Noah.

We find that man did not do too very well during this period of time—not well at all!

THE DISPENSATION OF GOVERNMENT

This dispensation lasted from Noah to Abraham, a period of about 400 years.

THE DISPENSATION OF PROMISE

At the time of Abraham, man entered into the dispensation of promise. This was due to the great promises made to Abraham as it regarded a number of things, but especially that of the coming Redeemer. This dispensation lasted about 400 years.

THE DISPENSATION OF LAW

At the time of Moses, mankind entered into the dispensation of law. This dispensation continued up unto the crucifixion and resurrection of Christ, which was a period of approximately 1,600 years.

THE DISPENSATION OF GRACE

Beginning on the day of Pentecost, mankind entered into the dispensation of grace, which continues unto this hour, a period thus far of about 2,000 years.

THE DISPENSATION OF RIGHTEOUSNESS

The next dispensation will be that of righteousness and will commence at the second coming and is labeled as the "kingdom age." It will last for 1,000 years.

THE DISPENSATION OF THE PERFECT AGE

The final dispensation, that is, if one could refer to that coming day in this fashion, is the dispensation of the perfect age. It will commence immediately after the kingdom age and will last forever. It is characterized in Revelation, Chapters 21 and 22.

Other than the final dispensation, declension, not progress, is stamped upon all. Each period opens hopefully but ends in judgment. Chapter 3 of Genesis narrates the ruin and judgment of the first dispensation.

THE FIRST TEMPTATION

The question, *"And he said unto the woman, Yes, has God said, You shall not eat of every tree of the garden?"* presents the beginning of the first temptation.

It begins with Satan twisting the Word of God, trying to make it say something that it did not really say. He did the same with Christ in the wilderness of temptation (Mat. 4:6). In fact, every single going astray of a human being is that he ignores the Word of God (as all unredeemed do), or else, he misinterprets the Word of God (as some Christians do). Admittedly, while it's not misinterpreted intentionally, the end result is the same.

An individual who is lost doesn't take the wrong road intentionally but irrespective of good intentions, he is still lost, and with negative results.

KNOWING THE BIBLE

That's the reason it's absolutely imperative for the believer to know and understand the Word of God. Knowing the Bible should be a lifelong project, and a person certainly can know it if he will apply himself. Unfortunately, most Christians presently little know the Word of God; consequently, they take the word of whatever preacher strikes them in a positive sense. In other words, they look on the outward, which is a poor way to judge the situation. In effect, they have placed their lives in the hands of that individual and are taking his word for whatever is done.

Untold millions are in hell right now because of this very thing. They didn't know the Word of God, and they took the word of somebody else, which proved to be wrong and caused them to be eternally lost. Nothing could be worse than that!

Remember this: Satan does not try to deny the Word as much as he tries to pervert the Word.

THE WOMAN

"And the woman said unto the serpent, We may eat of the fruit of the trees of the garden" (Gen. 3:2).

Through the serpent, Satan had addressed his question to the woman.

The woman answered the serpent, seemingly not surprised by the serpent's ability to speak. This shows that this animal evidently had at least some powers of limited speech.

In answering the question, she allowed that they may eat of the fruit of all the other trees of the garden, but not the fruit of the tree that was in the middle of the garden. She quoted what the Lord had said about the prohibition but then added, *"Neither shall you touch it."*

She reiterated the fact that the penalty for eating of this particular tree was death.

This proclaims Satan leveling his attack against Eve instead of Adam. To be sure, his use of Eve was only a means to get to Adam.

Had the fall stopped with Eve, which means that it would not have included Adam, the damage would have been confined to Eve. Due to the fact that it is the man who contains the seed of procreation, his partaking of the forbidden fruit would mean that not only would he fall, but the entirety of the human race that would follow after him would be fallen as well! In effect, all of humanity that would ever be born, with the exception of Jesus Christ, was in the loins of our first parent.

THE WOMAN WAS DECEIVED

Evidently Satan thought that Eve was the more susceptible to his suggestions. Concerning this incident, Paul said, *"And Adam was not deceived, but the woman being deceived was in the transgression"* (I Tim. 2:14).

Whatever Satan's reasons for using Eve to get to Adam, we learn from this, or at least we should, that the Evil One plays very, very dirty. Honesty and integrity are foreign to this fallen angel. That's the reason that if we attempt to match wits with him, even as Eve did, we, as well, will do the same as Eve.

In the matter of temptation, we are told to have no dialogue whatsoever with the Evil One, but rather, *"Submit yourselves therefore to God. Resist the Devil, and he will flee from you"* (James 4:7).

Peter also said, *"Be sober, be vigilant; because your adversary the Devil, as a roaring lion, walks about, seeking whom he may devour: Whom resist steadfast in the faith, knowing that the same afflictions are accomplished in your brethren who are in the world"* (I Pet. 5:8–9).

HOW DO WE RESIST THE DEVIL?

If most Christians had to answer this question, they would take their cue from Matthew, Chapter 4, concerning the temptation of Jesus in the wilderness. In other words, they would quote Scripture to Satan.

While the quoting of the Word of God is always good, that's not exactly what Jesus was doing as it regarded His temptation by the Evil One.

Jesus was answering Satan's suggestions by quoting what the Bible actually said about the matter, whatever it may have been. While one could certainly say that the Master's approach was definitely a resistance to Satan, more than anything else, it was a presentation of the proper perspective of the Word of God.

In fact, both James and Peter tell us how to resist the Devil. James told us first of all to submit ourselves therefore to God. Peter told us to resist the Evil One steadfast in the faith.

GOD'S WAY

When we submit ourselves to God as James said, we are, in effect, submitting ourselves to God's Word and way. What is that way?

That way is *"the faith,"* even as Peter stated (I Pet. 5:9). What is *the faith*?

In abbreviated form, the faith is *"Jesus Christ, and Him crucified"* (I Cor. 2:2). The idea is this: The believer is to have his faith placed exclusively in the Cross of Christ, which then guarantees the help of the Holy Spirit.

Listen to what Paul said: *"But if the Spirit* (Holy Spirit) *of Him* (God the Father) *who raised up Jesus from the dead dwell in you, He who raised up Christ from the dead shall also quicken your mortal bodies by His Spirit who dwells in you"* (Rom. 8:11).

The quickening of our mortal bodies by His Spirit that dwells in us does not refer to the coming resurrection, but rather speaks of power at this present time in order to overcome Satan and all temptation.

Paul also said, *"For the law of the Spirit of life in Christ Jesus has made me free from the law of sin and death"* (Rom. 8:2).

The words *"in Christ Jesus"* refer exclusively to what Christ did at the Cross on our behalf. When we place our faith in this finished work, the law of the Spirit of life in Christ Jesus is effected on our behalf. Trusting in the great sacrifice of Christ is properly resisting the Devil.

FORBIDDEN FRUIT

"We may eat of the fruit of the trees of the garden: But of the fruit of the tree which is in the midst of the garden, God has said, You shall not eat of it, neither shall you touch it, lest you die" (Gen. 3:2-3).

Verse 3 proclaims the fact that Eve very well knew the prohibition.

The trial of our first parents was ordained by God because probation was essential to their spiritual development and self-determination. However, as He did not desire that they should be tempted to their fall, the Lord would not suffer Satan to tempt them in a way that should surpass their human capacity. The tempted might, therefore, have resisted the tempter.

THE STRANGE WAYS OF TEMPTATION

Many scoff at the temptation of Eve simply because they do not understand the creation. A serpent who speaks seems to them but an idle tale, so they discount it as fable. But consider the following:

- The Bible is the Word of God, which means that every single word between the covers is true. As well, the Bible doesn't merely contain truth, it is truth. Inspiration guarantees the veracity not only of the thought but even down to the very word. In other words, the Holy Spirit literally searched through the vocabulary of Moses, as He did all other writers of the Sacred Text, until the right word was found, and then it was used as the lawgiver wrote the text.

- Before the fall, the creation was totally different than it is now. The idea that the serpent could speak seemed to pose no surprise for Eve; consequently, even as previously stated, it evidently had at least a limited ability to speak.

At any rate, Satan used the most unusual means by which to get the attention of Eve and ultimately Adam, which he evidently was able to do. Maybe we can say that in the case of every temptation, it comes in a most unusual manner, which is designed to carry forth its intended purpose.

What is that purpose? Satan wants you to believe a lie!

THE SERPENT SAID

"And the serpent said unto the woman, You shall not surely die" (Gen. 3:4).

As God had preached to Adam, Satan now preached to Eve. The object of Satan was to draw Eve away from that which God had said by what Satan said. His second step was to challenge the divine veracity. Jesus called Satan a liar, which probably referred to this very moment (Jn. 8:44).

The phrase, *"And the serpent said unto the woman,"* presents a position that has now gone terribly wrong. Eve should not have answered Satan when he spoke to her the first time. That was her first mistake.

I have to believe that along with her husband, Adam, Eve was of vast intelligence also. They had God as their teacher and however long that was, it was of monumental consequence, but despite all of that, she was now on the way to total deception.

This shows us that vast intelligence is not the answer. It does show us that obedience to the Word of God in every respect is the answer. Deception can only come about whenever we leave the Word, but the sad thing about the modern church is that it little knows the Word.

DENIAL OF THE WORD

The phrase, *"You shall not surely die,"* proclaims an outright denial of the Word of God but with a subtle twist, as we shall see in the next verse.

Among other things, this is probably what Jesus was referring to when He said to the Pharisees concerning Satan: *"You are of your father the Devil, and the lusts of your father you will do. He was a murderer from the beginning, and abode not in the truth, because there is no truth in him. When he speaks a lie, he speaks of his own: for he is a liar, and the father of it"* (Jn. 8:44).

What does he lie about? The answer is simple—everything!

So, in Eve's case, the moment she took herself out of the hands of God—out of the position of absolute dependence upon and subjection to His Word—she abandoned herself to the government of sense, as used of Satan for her entire overthrow.

THE ENTRANCE OF DEATH

God never intended for Adam and Eve, or any who would come after them, to die. By virtue of the Tree of Life, man was meant to live forever.

It was sin, i.e., the fall, that brought on death. The first type of death that occurred was separation from God, which was spiritual death.

With spiritual death having set in, the physical body was likewise affected. Due to the fact that man was driven out of the garden, therefore, unable to partake of the Tree of Life, physical death would ultimately occur. Even then, the physical body was so wondrously made that it took nearly 1,000 years for the first two or three generations to die.

All life comes from God, and with man cut off from God because of sin, man finds himself cut off from life.

It seems as if God did not explain all of this to Adam and Eve, but He rather just told them not to eat of the Tree of the Knowledge of Good and Evil. They were to obey without question.

However, the tragedy is, they did not obey, and in their disobedience, they found out the terrible truth that I have just briefly explained.

This was the knowledge that they sought, but to their chagrin, it was not to be what they thought.

YOUR EYES SHALL BE OPENED

"For God does know that in the day you eat thereof, then your eyes shall be opened, and you shall be as gods, knowing good and evil" (Gen. 3:5).

Satan accused God of lying.

The eyes being opened suggested the attainment of higher wisdom.

Satan told them they would be as Elohim.

At first Adam and Eve knew only good, but then, Satan said they would know both good and evil.

What was it about the evil that enticed her?

The phrase, *"For God does know that in the day you eat thereof, then your eyes shall be opened,"* presents the promise of the impartation of power to perceive physically, mentally, and spiritually objects that are not otherwise discernible. It suggests the attainment of higher wisdom, which, in effect, claims a higher wisdom than God. Unfortunately, Satan has not stopped peddling that lie from then until now, and worse yet, untold hundreds of millions, even billions, of souls have bought it.

Paul addressed this by saying, *"Professing themselves to be wise, they became fools"* (Rom. 1:22).

BLINDED EYES

The world was stunned and shocked by the senseless suicide attacks of the World Trade Center in New York City and the Pentagon in Washington, D.C., which took place

Sept. 11, 2001. Thousands lost their lives, and the sorrow of tens of thousands will be felt forever. As shocking and horrible as that was, however, the world is full of such activity, even on a daily basis, although on a smaller scale. It's all the result of the higher wisdom promised by Satan. That's why Jesus said, *"The thief comes not, but for to steal, and to kill, and to destroy: I am come that they might have life, and that they might have it more abundantly"* (Jn. 10:10).

The truth is, all eyes have been blinded as a result of the fall. They are opened only, and I mean only, as one accepts Christ as one's personal Saviour. This is what Jesus was talking about when He said, *"Except a man be born again, he cannot see the kingdom of God"* (Jn. 3:3).

As it regards the Islamic threat, there are several things we need to know, but, unfortunately, our leaders do not seem to know, and it is because they have believed a lie.

These things are:

- There is no such thing as a moderate Muslim. They all go by the Koran, and the Koran, to be brief, says, "Kill the infidel," and that is everyone who does not accept Islam.

- While all Muslims aren't murderers, all Muslims are definitely in sympathy with the murderers.

- The Muslims do not lack the will as it regards slaughter, and pertaining to the United States, they only lack the way.

- If the Muslims had the way to do it, the streets of every city and village in America would run red with blood.

- And yet, we have chosen to believe a lie, which claims that most Muslims are peace-loving people, with only a few who are labeled as radical. That's the big lie that we have believed.

- The Muslim world hates America, and they hate Israel. Israel is referred to as the little Satan, with America referred to as the great Satan.

- We have been led to believe that Muslims coming to America are doing so to search for a better life. That is not so! While there may be a few who would fall into that category, most are here (in the United States) to be of service to anyone who can weaken this nation.

- The Muslim religion is a religion of hate, murder, and thievery, in other words, a religion that is carried forth by demon spirits.

- Muslim children are taught to hate America and Israel from the time they are able to comprehend anything as little children.

The thing that would help America to a greater degree presently more than anything else is for a move of God to take place in the churches. Unfortunately, there doesn't seem to be any sign of such at present. The further away that people get from God (even those who call themselves Christians), the less they can recognize the lie. That's America's problem, and that's the problem of the modern church—the believing of a lie.

KNOWING GOOD AND EVIL

The phrase, *"And you shall be as gods, knowing good and evil,"* in effect, says, "You shall be as Elohim." It was a promise of divinity.

God is omniscient, meaning that He is all knowing; however, His knowledge of evil (and that knowledge is thorough) is not through personal experience. By His very nature, He is totally separate from all that is evil, and He hates it. The knowledge of evil that Eve would learn would be by moral degradation, which, of course, God never experienced and, in fact, could not experience. It would not be by intellectual insight that her ambitions would be fulfilled.

THE PROBLEM THAT PERSISTS

If we are to notice, whatever happened at the fall, and I speak of the temptations and even the manner of these temptations, lingers fully with man even unto this present hour. For instance, deception is a part and parcel of the human makeup. Man deceives others very easily and is deceived himself very easily. As well, there is an innate desire within man for that which is evil. That's at least one of the reasons for the terrible problems of drug addiction, etc. Young men and young women want to know how that forbidden fruit tastes.

Then we have the problem that has caused so many wars, privation, and want. I speak of man wanting to be God and, thereby, acting like God, but in a totally unlawful way. Such spirit characterizes all dictators and seemingly finds lodging in the hearts of all men.

So, we see how that deception, lies, and ungodly desires characterize the human race, and it all comes from the first temptation of our first parents. The lie that man believed is the lie that man is. The deception by which he was deceived is the deception by which he deceives. The unholy ambition that came upon his being is the unholy ambition that continues to drive him to eternal darkness.

EVIL

Let's first of all look at evil.

It is true that evil has an enticement that is unexplainable, except in the spiritual sense. However, evil could not have had an enticement to Eve, so the cause of her fall had to be a desire to be like God, but it was a desire to be like Him in an unlawful way.

Once the deed is done, and the nature of sin has implanted itself in the heart and life of the human being, then evil carries a great enticement. This enticement starts early, even with pre-teen children. That's the reason it's absolutely imperative that a child have godly parents to steer him in the right direction.

The utterly stupid idea of letting a child choose for himself (and stupid it is) is a sure road to destruction.

However, attached to all sin is also an enslaving bondage. Once it is entered into, the thrill of that sin is gone and even its enticement is gone, but by then, the victim is held in its clutches with an iron-like grip.

If the first cigarette isn't smoked, there will be no desire for the cigarette. If the first hit of drugs isn't taken, there will be no desire for drugs. In fact, the list is long and covers every facet of the warped passions of a fallen race.

Now, let's look at the good. Isn't good what it's all about? Yes, it is, but we find here that even good can be approached in the wrong way.

Once the evil was entered into, man then began to think that he could overcome the evil by doing good. That's the reason that Cain was so incensed when God wouldn't accept his sacrifice. The things he offered to God were the labor of his hands, on which he had expended much effort, and, as well, his offering was attractive. Inasmuch as it was good, why wouldn't God accept it?

So, the entirety of the human race, and I speak of the part that is unredeemed, thinks that doing good is the answer to the spiritual problem. In fact, almost all who are in hell at this particular moment are there because they believed this lie.

This is also the greatest problem that plagues the church. The answer to the entirety of humanity, whether redeemed or unredeemed, is the Cross of Christ. Everyone who is actually saved has embraced the Cross as it regards their initial salvation experience. Still, when it comes to sanctification, and we speak of becoming

Christlike and living this life on a daily basis, most Christians, as well, attempt to do all of this by doing good. Most do not look at it that way. In fact, they claim to be trusting Christ, but, nevertheless, that's exactly what most Christians are presently doing.

THE RESULT AND NEVER THE CAUSE

While doing good things is not wrong within itself and is actually right, the truth is, these things must be a result of our experience with the Lord and never the cause. Once we attempt to make them the cause, we then sin and sin greatly. We are, in effect, saying, whether we realize it or not, that what Jesus did at the Cross is insufficient and we must, therefore, add our personal efforts that we deem to be good (Gal. 6:14).

THE PREACHING OF THE CROSS

In 1997, the Lord began to open up to me the revelation of the Cross. He took me first of all to Romans, Chapter 6, and explained that particular chapter to me. He informed me that every single thing that we receive from God comes to us exclusively through the sacrifice of Christ. He then informed me that with that being the case, the object of my faith must always be Jesus Christ and Him crucified (I Cor. 1:23).

With that carried out, and continued to be carried out on a daily basis (Lk. 9:23), the Holy Spirit, who alone can make us what we ought to be, will then work mightily on our behalf (Rom. 8:1–11).

As the Lord was opening up this great subject more and more, even on a daily basis, I began to preach and teach it. I began to note the struggle that many Christians were having as they heard this great Message of the Cross. For almost all of them, they were hearing it for the first time.

THE GOOD PART OF THE TREE OF
THE KNOWLEDGE OF GOOD AND EVIL

Little by little I came to realize that the struggle was over this one thing called *good*. In other words, they took great pride in the good things they were doing, whatever those things may have been, and as Abraham was loath to give up Ishmael, they were loath to give up these good works. As stated, it was not that they should have stopped the doing of them. In fact, they should have done them even more, whatever they might have been. However, it was the trust, faith, and confidence they were putting in the doing of these things (thinking that it made them holy) that was so wrong. In other words, those things were and are the object of their faith. As such, whether they realize it or not, they have embraced the good part of the Tree of Knowledge of Good and Evil. Let the reader understand that whether it's the good part or the evil part, both are on the same tree, and both will bring the same result, which is destruction.

The poor sinner coming to Christ is able to be saved only because of what Jesus did at the Cross. Likewise, the believer attempting to live this Christian life can do so only by what Jesus did at the Cross. But yet, it seems just as hard for the believer to embrace the Cross in order to be sanctified as it is for the sinner to be saved.

THE LUST OF THE EYES

"And when the woman saw that the tree was good for food, and that it was pleasant to the eyes, and a tree to be desired to make one wise, she took of the fruit thereof, and did eat, and gave also unto her husband with her; and he did eat" (Gen. 3:6).

This presents to us the first step of the three steps that lead ever downward. The apostle John mentioned this, *"For all that is in the world, the lust of the flesh, and the lust of the eyes, and the pride of life, is not of the Father, but is of the world"* (I Jn. 2:16).

If we are to notice, the lust of the eyes came first with Eve, while the lust of the flesh was presented first by John. Why the disparity?

Eve had no lust of the flesh at this stage. She was pure and innocent. So, the first assault to her at this time had to be the lust of the eyes, which would then be followed by the other two.

Once man had fallen, the lust of the flesh is always first and is followed by the lust of the eyes and the pride of life. This is the pattern! It more or less sets the stage for all spiritual failure.

DAVID

David's problem is a perfect example, even as recorded in II Samuel, Chapter 11. The lust of the flesh was already prevalent in David because of a lax spiritual condition.

He then *"saw a woman washing herself; and the woman was very beautiful to look upon"* (II Sam. 11:2), which constitutes the lust of the eyes. The lust of the flesh is already prevalent, so the lust of the eyes comes easily.

The Scripture then says, *"And David sent messengers, and took her; and she came in unto him, and he lay with her,"* which constitutes the pride of life (II Sam. 11:4). This pride of life says, "I am king, and it makes no difference that she is married to another man. If I want her, I will take her."

In one way or the other, this is more or less the pattern of all sin.

As stated, at this time, Eve, having no lust of the flesh, came to failure first of all by the lust of the eyes when she saw that the tree was good for food.

In the first place, she had no business even being around the tree. There were all types of trees in the garden, bearing all manner of fruits, which were available to her at any time. However, at the bidding of the Evil One, she succumbed to his suggestions, and then she minutely inspected this Tree of the Knowledge of Good and Evil.

THE LUST OF THE FLESH

The phrase, *"And that it was pleasant to the eyes,"* constitutes the lust of the flesh.

However, let us state that the entirety of this ungodly trio—the lust of the eyes, the lust of the flesh, and the pride of life—was all outward at this stage as it regarded Eve, whereas they are all inward following the fall. Nevertheless, even from an outward position, they were lethal. If they were lethal even from an outward position, how much more deadly are they inwardly! Then her eyes saw this fruit, and her flesh wanted it.

As stated, at the present time, it is a little different: since the fall, the flesh wants it, and when the eyes see it, the victim is pretty much helpless because of the pride of life.

THE PRIDE OF LIFE

"And a tree to be desired to make one wise" (Gen. 3:6).

This presents the pride of life.

Pride is, no doubt, the foundation sin of all sins. It is the bottom line regarding what caused the fall. In reality, Eve had no pride of life before she fell, but she did see the potential of such. It was the potential that dragged her down, i.e., to be like God, but to be like Him in an unlawful way.

Pride is the reason the sinner refuses to come to Christ or even admit his need for Christ. Pride is also the reason the Christian doesn't walk in victory. This pride makes him think that he can live this life without subscribing to God's order, which is the Cross.

THE FRUIT

"She took of the fruit thereof, and did eat" (Gen. 3:6).

This constitutes the fall. It was not that there was some type of chemical in the fruit that caused the problem, but rather disobedience to God. In effect, she was saying, as all who sin say, that she was smarter than God.

From that moment, billions have continued to take *"of the fruit thereof, and eat."* Exactly as Eve found, they have found that it didn't bring, and it doesn't bring, that which is supposed.

HER HUSBAND

"And gave also unto her husband with her; and he did eat" (Gen. 3:6).

This refers to the fact that evidently Adam was an observer to all these proceedings. With that being the case, he lifted no hand or voice to stop Eve from this terrible thing. Some claim that he ate of the forbidden fruit that she offered him out of love for her. Let me answer that in this way: No one ever sins out of love, so the reason he did this thing is even worse than her sin. She was deceived, but the Scripture plainly says, *"Adam was not deceived"* (I Tim. 2:14).

While he yielded to the temptation, he did not do so out of deception. So, the only reason we can give as to why he did this thing is that he entered into unbelief. At that time, he did not exactly believe what God had said about this situation. So, he took of the fruit and did eat, and when he did, he died instantly. We refer to spiritual death, which means separation from God.

THE SIN NATURE

The sin nature is that, after the fall, man's nature is to sin. Every thought he thinks, every step he takes, and everything he does is toward sin! His human nature is corrupted by the sin nature.

To describe the sin nature, one could say that it is the *"lust of the flesh, and the lust of the eyes, and the pride of life"* (I Jn. 2:16).

All unsaved people have two natures: human nature and the sin nature.

All believers have three natures: human nature, the divine nature, and the sin nature. However, the sin nature in the life of the believer is supposed to be dormant. The Scripture doesn't tell us that the sin nature is dead, but it does tell us that we are dead to the sin nature, or rather should be (Rom. 6:11).

WHILE THE SIN NATURE DOES DWELL IN THE BELIEVER, IT IS NOT TO RULE OR REIGN

Some 17 times in Romans, Chapter 6, Paul uses the word *sin*. Fourteen times out of the 17, the original Greek carries what is referred to as the definite article before the word *sin*. Consequently, it actually says *"the* sin.*"*

This means that Paul is not talking about a specific act of sin, but rather the sin nature, which, if not controlled properly, will definitely lead to acts of sin.

The unbeliever is controlled by the sin nature, but believers are definitely not to be controlled in this manner.

Paul said, *"Let not* (the) *sin therefore reign in your mortal body, that you should obey it in the lusts thereof"* (Rom. 6:12). This means that while the sin nature does dwell in the believer, it is not to rule or reign.

Some preachers claim that the believer no longer has a sin nature. If this is so, why was Paul addressing this subject repeatedly?

He was addressing it simply because the Christian does have a sin nature, and if he doesn't approach it in the correct way, he will find this terrible sin nature once again ruling and reigning in his life exactly as it did before he was saved. In fact, one can probably say without fear of contradiction that, sadly and regrettably, this is the case with most Christians.

Why?

THE CROSS OF CHRIST

If the believer doesn't understand the Message of the Cross, which is God's prescribed order of victory, the believer will be pretty well helpless to be what he ought to be, no matter how hard he tries otherwise. This means that the works of the flesh will be dominant in his life in some way (Gal., Chpt. 5).

GOD'S PRESCRIBED ORDER OF VICTORY

God has one means of salvation, and that is the Cross of Christ. He has one means of sanctification, and that is the Cross of Christ. The Cross alone is God's answer to sin. If we forget that, then we are missing completely God's prescribed order of victory.

The following has already been given, but due to the seriousness of the matter, please allow the repetition:

- Jesus Christ is the source. This means that our Lord is the source of all blessings that we receive from God the Father (Jn. 1:1-3, 14; 14:6, 20).

- The Cross of Christ is the means. This means that every-thing was made possible by the Cross. The price that Jesus there paid, which was the sacrifice of Himself, sat-isfied the demands of a thrice-holy God. Without the Cross, our Lord is *"another Jesus"* (II Cor. 11:4). It was the Cross of Christ that made and makes everything possible. It was there that the price was paid and, of course, when we speak of the Cross, we aren't speaking of the wooden beam on which Jesus died, but rather what He there did (Rom. 6:1-14; Col. 2:10-15).

- The Cross, the object of our faith. Inasmuch as Jesus is the source of all things we receive from God, and inas-much as the Cross is the means by which these things come to us, it is imperative that the Cross of Christ be the object of our faith. Christ and the Cross is what made everything possible, and it demands our faith. The story of the Bible is the story of Jesus Christ and Him crucified (I Cor. 1:17, 18, 23; 2:2; Col. 2:14-15).

- The Holy Spirit. With our understanding that Christ is the source, the Cross is the means, and the Cross of Christ is the object of our faith, the Holy Spirit, who works exclusively within the parameters of the finished work of Christ, will work mightily on our behalf. This is the way the Holy Spirit works. He will not work any other way. He demands that our faith be exclusively in Christ and the Cross (Rom. 8:1-11; Eph. 2:13-18).

WALKING AFTER THE SPIRIT—
WALKING AFTER THE FLESH

What we've just given you in these previous points is actually the meaning of walking after the Spirit and walking after the flesh.

Paul said, *"There is therefore now no condemnation to them which are in Christ Jesus, who walk not after the flesh, but after the Spirit"* (Rom. 8:1).

The Spirit of God always leads to Christ and His Cross. Consequently, the first point we gave you constitutes walking after the Spirit.

If we devise other means, which, in effect, refers to one looking to self instead of Christ and the Cross, such constitutes walking after the flesh.

Many Christians think that walking after the Spirit refers to doing spiritual things, whatever those things might be. It doesn't!

They also think that walking after the flesh refers to doing carnal things, such as watching too much television, etc. None of that is correct!

Walking after the Spirit constitutes one placing one's faith totally in Christ and what Christ has done for us at the Cross (Rom. 8:2).

Walking after the flesh constitutes the believer looking elsewhere other than the Cross, in other words, to his own ability, strength, and machinations. It has nothing to do with watching too much television, being too interested in sports, etc.

Once again we state the truth that the Cross of Christ is the only answer for hurting humanity, whether the unredeemed or the redeemed.

OPEN EYES

"And the eyes of them both were opened, and they knew that they were naked; and they sewed fig leaves together, and made themselves aprons" (Gen. 3:7).

"And the eyes of them both were opened" refers to the consciousness of guilt as a result of their sin.

Sin makes the most excellent and glorious of all God's creatures vile and shameful. It defaces the image of God. It separates man from God. It disorders all the faculties of the soul.

Once this thing was done, the promised results came, but it was not what they thought it would be. Instead of it making them like gods, it showed them that they were like beasts and brought the first sense of shame.

The first thing that their opened eyes saw was themselves, and the immediate result of the sight was the first blush of shame.

NAKED

"And they knew that they were naked," refers to the fact that they had lost the enswathing light of purity, which previously had clothed their bodies. They were shamed before God and angels, disgraced in the highest degree, and laid open to the

contempt and reproach of heaven and earth and their own consciousnesses. Sin is a reproach to any people!

THE JUDGMENT OF GOD

The word *naked,* as presented here, has more to do with their being naked to the judgment of God than it does an absence of clothing. God cannot abide sin, and sin must be judged.

Of course, we know, and as we shall see, God provided for this judgment by the giving of His only Son, who took the judgment for us. However, if Christ is refused, there remains no more sacrifice for sin, and judgment must inevitably fall (Heb. 10:12, 26).

FIG LEAVES

"And they sewed fig leaves together, and made themselves aprons," presents the clothing Adam and Eve provided for themselves, which did very well until God appeared, but the fig leaves were then found to be worthless. Sinners clothe themselves with morality, sacraments, and religious ceremony. They are as worthless as Adam's apron of fig leaves.

In this we see true Christianity and mere religion. The former is founded upon the fact of a person being clothed, of course, with the robe of righteousness; the latter is founded upon the fact of him being naked. The former has this as its starting ground, while the latter has it as its goal. All that a true Christian does is because he is clothed with the robe of righteousness.

This is made possible by Christ and what Christ did at the Cross, and it is imputed to believing sinners upon faith in the finished work of Christ. All that religion does is in order for him to be clothed. In other words, the person is working for his salvation, while the former is working because of his salvation.

The more we examine man's religion and all its phases, the more we shall see its thorough insufficiency to remedy his state.

Incidentally, religion is that which is devised totally by man, which claims to reach God or to better oneself in some way. It is not of God and, thereby, cannot be sanctioned by God. That which is of God is totally of God and not at all of man.

MAN'S CONDITION

We're looking here at man's condition and how this condition can be rectified.

Man knows that he is *"naked."* He may not like to admit it, and many may even deny it, but he knows! The question is, "How is his condition remedied?"

Man has a choice, and it's not really a very complex choice to make. The only way his situation can be remedied is by his acceptance of Christ, and more particularly, what Christ did for him at the Cross. If he does that, he will find that a perfect, pure, and spotless righteousness will be imputed unto him, and done so instantly. The situation is then resolved.

However, if he refuses God's remedy and resorts to fig leaves, which, regrettably and sadly, characterizes much of the world for all time, he will find himself continuing to be naked.

If man has a problem, and this problem seems to affect all, it's the problem of the *"fig leaves."*

COVERING

The following is an actual happening. It is simple and silly, but it adequately defines, I think, that of which I speak.

Donnie was preaching a meeting in a particular state some time ago. After he had been there a day or so, the pastor asked him, "Who is your covering?"

At first Donnie didn't know what he was meaning, and the preacher, seeing the puzzled look on his face, further explained, "A preacher or preachers who vouch for your integrity."

While the laity would have little knowledge of this, it is big, especially among Charismatic and Pentecostal preachers. Along the same vein, the preachers associated with denominations think of their particular denominations as their covering.

Donnie answered, saying, "The blood of Jesus Christ is my covering." He then went on to say, "I'm really not interested in what some preacher might say about me, and for the simple reason, as Adam of old, he really cannot even cover his own backside."

I'll be frank with you, I liked the answer!

This is just one of the fig leaves that characterizes a whole forest of such.

I want my brother in the Lord to speak well of me. In fact, I want all believers to speak well of me; however, whatever it is they do say really won't amount to that much in the final analysis. It's what God knows that counts. To be frank, people say things about me, and God says things about me. It's really only what God says that actually matters.

THE VOICE OF THE LORD GOD

"And they heard the voice of the LORD *God walking in the garden in the cool of the day: and Adam and his wife hid themselves from the presence of the* LORD *God amongst the trees of the garden"* (Gen. 3:8).

The voice of the Lord had heretofore been a pleasant sound. Now it was the very opposite. Whereas the sound of His voice had once been a sound of delight, it was now a sound of dread, fear, and even stark terror.

It is not that the voice of the Lord had changed, for it hadn't. It was the same voice that they had heard since creation. He hadn't changed, but they had.

Paul wrote, quoting David, *"Today if you will hear His voice, harden not your hearts"* (Heb. 4:7; Ps. 95:7–8).

We find in this that the Lord seeks the sinner. Actually, He seeks the sinner to a far greater degree than we could begin to imagine. That's why He came down to this earth, took upon Himself human flesh, and did so in order that He might die on a Cross that the debt could be paid—a debt, incidentally, that we could not pay no matter what we did.

He is still saying: *"Come unto Me, all you who labor and are heavy laden, and I will give you rest. Take My yoke upon you, and learn of Me; for I am meek and lowly in heart: and ye shall find rest unto your souls. For My yoke is easy, and My burden is light"* (Mat. 11:28–30).

He's still saying, *"Come unto Me!"*

GUILT

"And Adam and his wife hid themselves from the presence of the LORD God amongst the trees of the garden" (Gen. 3:8).

This presents our first parents hiding themselves, not in humility as unworthy to come into God's presence or through modesty, but rather from a sense of guilt.

One commentary says, "Here is the dawn of a new era in the history of humanity. The eye of a guilty conscience is now opened for the first time, and God and the universe appear in new and terrible forms."[1]

It played out to an alarming dread of God, but yet, there's no way to flee from God because God is everywhere, i.e., omnipresent. So, we find that guilt blinds the reason of men.

Christ alone can remove the guilt, which is done instantly upon acceptance of Him as one's Lord and Saviour. Paul said, *"There is therefore now no condemnation to them which are in Christ Jesus, who walk not after the flesh, but after the Spirit"* (Rom. 8:1).

The Greek scholars say that this verse can be translated, *"There is therefore now no guilt to them which are in Christ Jesus."*

THE FALL

The unredeemed don't know what it is to be without guilt; consequently, they cannot imagine living without this terrible malady.

Guilt plays a tremendous part in all suicides, nervous breakdowns, and emotional disturbances, and is actually a factor in every adverse thing that happens to a human being. However, not ever having experienced a time without guilt, the unredeemed have no idea what a guilt-free life actually is. It is the most wonderful, glorious, and fulfilling lifestyle that one could ever enjoy, but the unredeemed have no concept of what that means. It's what Jesus was speaking of when He said, *"I am come that they might have life, and that they might have it more abundantly"* (Jn. 10:10).

With the fall of our first parents, guilt came into the physical, mental, and spiritual makeup of all individuals. As stated, it is not possible for it to be removed except by the acceptance of Jesus Christ as one's Lord and Saviour. We must never forget that what Christ does for us was all made possible by the Cross (Gal. 2:20–21; 6:14; Eph. 2:6–18; Col. 2:14–15).

THE CALL

"And the LORD God called unto Adam, and said unto him, Where are you?" (Gen. 3:9).

"And the LORD God called unto Adam," presents God seeking the first man. He has been doing so ever since.

Matthew Henry said: "This inquiry after Adam may be looked upon as a gracious pursuit, in kindness to him, and in order to his recovery. If God had not called to him, to reclaim him, his condition had been as desperate as that of fallen angels."[2]

He went on to say, "This lost sheep had wandered endlessly, if the Good Shepherd had not sought after him, to bring him back, and in order to do that, reminded him where he was not, where he should not be, and where he could not be either happy or easy."³

The Lord called to Adam, and He has been calling to untold millions of others ever since.

WHERE ARE YOU?

"And said unto him, Where are you?" presents the question of all questions. To be sure, the Lord knew exactly where Adam was, but He wanted Adam to know where he was.

Williams says: "Adam hides from God, not because of any change in God, but because of the change in himself, wrought by the entrance of sin. The covering he provided for himself did very well until God appeared and was then found to be worthless."⁴

Adam's absence was clear proof that something was wrong. Before this, he had welcomed the divine approach, but now, there was dread and fear.

Every believer should take to heart this question asked by our heavenly Father so long ago, *"Where are you?"*

As we've already stated, God knows where each of us is. Being omniscient (all-knowing), He knows everything about us, but oftentimes, we don't know ourselves exactly where we are. It takes that clarion call to bring us to our senses!

FEAR

"And he said, I heard Your voice in the garden, and I was afraid, because I was naked; and I hid myself" (Gen. 3:10).

"And he said, I heard Your voice in the garden, and I was afraid," presents the first words that came out of the mouth of our first parent after the fall. He said, *"I was afraid."* Why was he afraid?

Concerning this moment, Calvin said, "His consciousness of the effects of sin was keener than his sense of the sin itself."[5]

Lange said, "This is the first instance of that mingling and confusion of sin and punishment which is the peculiar characteristic of our redemption-needing humanity."[6]

Luther said: "The words, 'Where are you?' are words of divine law, directed by God to Adam's conscience. God wanted Adam to know that he who hides himself from Him is never hidden from Him, and that he who runs away from Him can never escape Him."

The type of fear that characterized Adam was fear brought on by guilt. That's why guilt is such a hazard—it carries with it a tremendous amount of negative baggage.

TAKE IT TO JESUS

This type of fear sees God in a completely erroneous way. It sees Him as someone to be dreaded and someone to be avoided, but let the reader understand this: Sin is a horrible business, actually, the cause of all sorrow, heartache, and destruction in this world, and, as well, it always brings heavy guilt; however, sin should be taken to the Lord, as distasteful and shameful as it might be. There's no one else who can do anything about one's sin except the Lord of Glory, and His answer for sin is the Cross, which is the greatest example of love that humanity has ever known.

God forbid that we fail the Lord in any capacity; however, regrettably and sadly, the sin problem plagues the whole of the human race, even the godliest at times. As bad as it might be and as shameful as it might be, as the great song says:

Take it to Jesus, take it to Jesus,
He is a friend that's well-known.

The great mistake made by the human race and, regrettably, even by the church, is that we take the sin elsewhere. We take it to the psychologist, who, to be blunt (and I mean to be blunt), can do nothing! We take it to fellow human beings, and no matter how godly they may be, still, they can do nothing.

Beautifully and wondrously, John the Beloved told us what to do: *"If we confess our sins, He is faithful and just to forgive us our sins, and to cleanse us from all unrighteousness"* (I Jn. 1:9).

RESTORATION

The ministry of restoration should be the ministry of every believer. Sooner or later, each believer will be called upon to aid a brother or sister in distress. I speak of one who has failed the Lord.

Paul told us what to do in such a case: *"Brethren, if a man be overtaken in a fault, you who are spiritual, restore such an one in the spirit of meekness; considering yourself, lest you also be tempted"* (Gal. 6:1).

So, what did he mean by this statement?

There is only one way that one can be restored. The one who is spiritual is to explain to the individual who has failed these two things:

1. Why he failed

2. What to do so as not to fail again

To say that one is spiritual means that this particular individual knows and understands God's prescribed order of victory, which is the Cross.

The one who is spiritual should patiently explain to the brother or sister that he or she has failed because of taking his or her eyes off the Cross and, thereby, shifting his or her faith to other things, which is what caused the problem to begin with. When this was done, the Holy Spirit simply would not help the believer because He will not work outside of the parameters of the finished work of Christ. Consequently, such a person becomes an open target for Satan.

While he might try with all of his strength to overcome, he will find that despite all of his efforts, he has failed.

CONFUSION

This is generally very confusing to such a Christian. He doesn't understand why he has failed simply because he has tried so hard. In fact, he didn't want to do what was done and tried not to do it but found himself in the same condition as

Paul before he knew the victory of the Cross. He said, *"For that which I do I allow* (understand) *not: for what I would, that do I not; but what I hate, that do I"* (Rom. 7:15).

For a Christian to be in such a state and then for a fellow Christian to berate him or seek to punish him in some way only adds insult to injury.

What good would it have done to have ridiculed Paul or to have punished him when he was in the Romans, Chapter 7, state? Regrettably, that's what many Christians seek to do.

Please understand, as well, that God doesn't have two remedies for sin—one for the laity and another for preachers. The remedy is all the same, which is the Cross.

Once the failing one has been told why he failed, which was a departure from the Cross, he is to then be told to get his faith back to the Cross and keep the Cross as the object of his faith from then on. This will guarantee victory ahead simply because the Holy Spirit will now help him.

This is the manner in which restoration is to be enjoined, and that is the only manner that restoration can be enjoined (Rom. 6:3–14; 8:1-11).

THE CHRISTIAN AND SIN

If a Christian is truly born again, that person hates sin. While the flesh may want something that is sin, the inward man doesn't (Rom. 7:22). So, the following is what we have: *"For that which I do I allow not* (I understand not)*: for what I would, that do I not; but what I hate, that do I"* (Rom. 7:15).

Not understanding the Message of the Cross, most Christians presently (I speak of those who truly love the Lord) find themselves in the same position that Paul found himself before the Holy Spirit showed him the victory of the Cross. The life that Paul wanted to live, which was that of godliness, he found that he couldn't. That which he hated, which was failure, he found himself doing. As stated, that's exactly where most modern Christians find themselves.

THE CHRISTIAN AND WILLPOWER

Most Christians have the erroneous idea that once they're saved, the Lord gives them a super will to where they can say no to the Devil, etc. That is basely incorrect. The will of the believer is no different than the will of the unbeliever.

While the will is important—*"whosoever will"*—still, the believer cannot live a victorious life by the power of his will. While he certainly has to will to do such, that's as far as it goes. Sadly, that's where most Christians are. They are trying to live for God by the means of willpower, which cannot be done. If it could, then Jesus would not have had to come down here and die on a Cross.

Here is something that the believer should understand, although most will deny what they read here, but it happens to be the truth: If the believer is functioning according to the strength of his willpower, he will find that Satan can override his will and force him into doing something that he doesn't want to do. In fact, it happens millions of times every day all over the world.

Let's listen again to what Paul said about the will: *"For I know that in me (that is, in my flesh,) dwells no good thing: for to will is present with me* (willpower); *but how to perform that which is good I find not"* (Rom. 7:18).

Clearly and plainly, the apostle here tells us that he had the will to do that which was right, but despite having the proper will, he still couldn't do what was right. Please understand, and again we state, that's where most modern believers are. They are trying to live for God by means of willpower but simply are unable to do so.

Let's quote Paul again: *"For I delight in the law of God after the inward man: But I see another law in my members, warring against the law of my mind, and bringing me into captivity to the law of sin which is in my members"* (Rom. 7:22-23).

WHAT IS THE PROPER WAY TO LIVE FOR GOD?

The only answer for sin is the Cross of Christ. That's where Jesus atoned for all sin—past, present, and future—at least for all who will believe (Col. 2:14-15). This means that at Calvary, Satan, plus all demon spirits and fallen angels, were totally and completely defeated. So, the answer is the Cross.

However, as we've already stated in this volume, for the believer to have the help of the Holy Spirit—help which we cannot do without—he is going to have to understand that his victory is in the Cross of Christ, which means that everything else is laid aside.

Listen again to Paul: *"For Christ sent me not to baptize, but to preach the gospel: not with wisdom of words, lest the Cross of Christ should be made of none effect"* (I Cor. 1:17).

In this one verse of Scripture, the Holy Spirit through Paul tells us what the gospel of Jesus Christ really is—it is the Cross of Christ.

One can say it this way: Jesus is the new covenant. This doesn't mean that He *has* the new covenant, but rather that He *is* the new covenant. The Cross of Christ is the meaning of that new covenant, meaning that if you do not understand the Cross relative to sanctification, then you really don't know what the new covenant actually is.

The Lord gave Paul the meaning of the new covenant, which is the Cross, and the great apostle gave it to us in his 14 epistles.

In I Corinthians 1:17, the Lord is telling us that nothing must stand in the way of the Cross. As important as water baptism is, it must not be used as the means of life, living, and victory. That is the domain of the Cross and the Cross alone.

The Holy Spirit is God, who can do anything. He works exclusively within the parameters of the finished work of Christ. When the believer places his or her faith exclusively in Christ and the Cross, then the Holy Spirit will work mightily on behalf of the believer.

HIDING FROM GOD

"Because I was naked; and I hid myself" (Gen. 3:10).

Such presents a foolish effort.

Luther said, "From this we learn how great is the evil of sin. Unless God helps and calls the sinner, he will forever flee God, try to excuse his sin by lies, and add one wrong to another until he ends in blasphemy and despair."

How foolish it is to seek to hide from God. God knows all things, so to hide from Him is impossible. He had heard the voice of God in the garden and said that it made him afraid, but had he not heard God's voice when He had commanded him not to eat of the forbidden tree? Why was he not afraid of God then, and why did he not hide himself at that time?

Believe it or not, men are still seeking to hide themselves from God; however, they do it in strange ways.

Many will not go to church at all because they surmise that God is in church and that He will then apprehend them. They don't seem to realize that God is everywhere.

DAVID

Concerning God, David said:

O LORD, You have searched me, and known me. You know my downsitting and my uprising, You understand my thoughts afar off. You compass my path and my lying down, and are acquainted with all my ways. For there is not a word in my tongue, but, lo, O LORD, You know it altogether. You have beset me behind and before, and laid Your hand upon me. Such knowledge is too wonderful for me; it is high, I cannot attain unto it. Where shall I go from Your Spirit? or where shall I flee from Your presence? If I ascend up into heaven, You are there: if I make my bed in hell, behold, You are there. If I take the wings of the morning, and dwell in the uttermost parts of the sea; Even there shall Your hand lead me, and Your right hand shall hold me. If I say, Surely the darkness shall cover me; even the night shall be light about me. Yes, the darkness hides not from You; but the night shines as the day: the darkness and the light are both alike to You (Ps. 139:1–12).

NAKED

We have already addressed ourselves to this, but it is here that the idea seems to project itself that before the fall, Adam and Eve had been enveloped in light. With the fall, the light disappeared, and they were left naked. Let us say again that which we have already stated: The word *naked* here carries a far greater connotation than merely being without clothing. They were naked to the judgment of God.

Luther said, not necessarily relating to this one incident, but rather the overall picture, but yet, the particulars are the same: "When Moses says that God called Adam, this means that He hailed him before His judgment seat. Eve, too, had sinned and fallen from God so that she also was summoned and had to share in this judgment."

THE JUDGMENT OF GOD

This is the main problem: Men are concerned about the judgment of God, and rightly so! Let it ever be known and understood that God cannot tolerate sin in any shape, form, or fashion. Sin must be judged wherever it is found.

Now, the Lord has a glorious and wonderful solution for that—His Son, the Lord Jesus Christ and the price that He paid on the Cross. In other words, Christ took the judgment that the whole of humanity should have suffered.

So, man has a choice: He can accept God's Son, with all judgment being suspended, for the simple reason that it is not proper to punish for the same crime twice. Jesus has suffered the stroke of God, which is death, all on our behalf, which paid the terrible sin debt. When He said, *"It is finished,"* that meant the debt was forever paid. So, if the believing sinner accepts Christ, there is no fear of judgment, and there will never be any fear of judgment.

However, if the sinner refuses Christ, the wrath of God remains on him; one can be certain of that. So, the die is cast; we either accept Christ or suffer the judgment of God.

PSYCHOLOGY

Modern man has tried to answer the sure judgment of God by denying it. In fact, the world has been so psychologized that it no longer believes there will be a judgment.

Psychology teaches that man is inherently good, and if he does something wrong, it is because of outside environment or events beyond his control. So, in this teaching, no person is ever guilty, but rather society, environment, other people, etc. are to blame. In this type of thinking, there can be no judgment because there is no culpability on the part of the individual.

The Bible teaches the very opposite. It teaches that all men are sinful and wicked as a result of the fall. It teaches that man is responsible for his actions and will have to ultimately answer to God, i.e., the judgment (Rom. 1:18; Rev. 20:11-15).

WHY THE GUILT?

So, it doesn't really matter what crutch man leans on; the Word of God will prevail, and man will ultimately answer. As well, if man is not personally guilty, as psychology claims, then why is he plagued with guilt?

Psychology claims that the Bible is responsible for that. So, if the Bible could be banned, this would stop the guilt, they say. What they should understand is that the Bible doesn't make the guilt, but it only points out what is already there. Man is not guilty merely because the Bible says he's guilty, but he is guilty because, in fact, that's what he is. The guilt is a result of his sinful state. However, let it be understood that the Bible not only points out the problem, but it also points out the solution, who is Christ and Him crucified (Jn. 3:3, 16; Eph. 6:18; Col. 2:10–15).

THE FIRST QUESTION

"And He said, Who told you that you were naked? Have you eaten of the tree, whereof I commanded you that you should not eat?" (Gen. 3:11).

This question, *"And he said, Who told you that you were naked?"* carries Adam's mind from the effect to the sin that had caused it. As long as a man feels sorrow only for the results of his action, there is no repentance and no wish to return to the divine presence.

What he had described as a want or imperfection, which was his being naked, was really the result of his own act.

Adam was afraid because he was naked. He was not only unarmed, therefore, afraid to contend with God, but also unclothed and therefore afraid to even appear before Him. We have reason to be afraid of approaching God if we are not clothed and fenced with the righteousness of God; that alone will be armor of proof and cover the shame of our nakedness.

However, the sin has grown worse, as all sin grows worse. While Adam did admit that he was naked, untold millions presently deny being naked even though they obviously are. Adam did hide from God, or rather tried to do so, but man presently doesn't even actually try to hide. He brazenly confronts God, of which we see the type in Chapter 4 as it regards the actions of Cain.

THE SECOND QUESTION

"Have you eaten of the tree, whereof I commanded you that you should not eat?" is the question, and the answer is carried with the question. That is exactly what Adam and Eve had done! They had eaten of the tree whereof the Lord commanded that they should not partake.

It is not so much the occasion of the sin of which the Lord inquired, but of the consciousness of nakedness that is addressed here. The Lord then asked the question that points to the true cause of the man's nakedness, which, of course, proclaimed the divine knowledge of the transgression.

The way the question is framed removes the pretext of ignorance, and also points to the fact that the sin had been carried out in direct violation of the divine prohibition.

ADAM SAID

"And the man said, The woman whom You gave to be with me, she gave me of the tree, and I did eat" (Gen. 3:12).

"And the man said," is that which Adam said, and it proclaims the course of action that would be taken. Adam then and there could have confessed his sin but chose another route. Consequently, there is no record in the Word of God that he ever fully made things right with the Lord. He is not listed in Hebrews, Chapter 11, along with the great faith worthies, and more than likely, he died lost.

There are some who claim that his tomb is in Jerusalem. There is another rumor which claims that his body was placed in the ark along with Noah and his family at the time of the flood. Actually, the rumor claims that his coffin is still in the ark where it is ensconced on Mount Ararat.

We can get an idea of what God intended for this man (our first parent) to be by the Holy Spirit through Paul referring to Jesus as the *"last Adam"* (I Cor. 15:45).

THE EXCUSE

"The woman whom You gave to be with me, she gave me of the tree, and I did eat," indicates, it seems, that Adam now had

little sense of responsibility, and no feeling that he had a duty toward Eve and ought to have watched over her and helped her when tempted.

He, in effect, blamed God for his predicament. He, in fact, insinuated that God was accessory to his sin! God gave him the woman, and she gave him the fruit. So, in a secondary way, he blamed Eve also!

It is strange that man wants to be like God but, as stated, in an unlawful way, and then when things go wrong, he wants to blame God. He seems to forget that if he is like God, he will have to take responsibility for his actions.

WHAT DOES IT MEAN TO TAKE RESPONSIBILITY?

As we are speaking here of sin, we will address ourselves to that particular problem.

To fail the Lord is an extremely hurtful thing, as should be obvious. In the event of failure, what can one do, and to be more particular, what should one do according to the Word of God as it regards taking responsibility? That's the key—the Word of God!

The failing Christian is to confess his sins to the Lord. If he has sinned against particular individuals, he has to confess his wrongdoing to them, as well, otherwise, only to God. Upon proper confession of sin, the Scripture plainly says that Christ will be *"faithful and just to forgive us our sins, and to cleanse us from all unrighteousness"* (I Jn. 1:9).

As well, the believer is to understand that he has failed because he has allowed his faith to be shifted from the Cross of Christ to other things. When this happens, the Holy Spirit will not help such a believer, and he is then left to the mercy of his own strength and ability, which are woefully insufficient as it regards the powers of darkness.

So, he is to once again get his faith anchored in the great sacrifice of Christ and look to the finished work, which means to place his faith and confidence exclusively in what Christ has done for him at the Cross. Doing this, the Holy Spirit will once again begin to help him, and he will walk again in victory (Rom. 8:1–2, 11).

WRONG DIRECTION

Unfortunately, there are many in the modern church who claim that taking responsibility means that one must submit oneself to whatever foolish rules and regulations that silly men make up, which are totally unscriptural. In other words, they're speaking of punishment.

Let the reader understand that those who advocate punishment in such a case had best first look at themselves. As well, they had best understand that by their actions, they are, in fact, saying that what Jesus suffered at the Cross was not enough, and more punishment needs to be added. Such, to be sure, is abominable in the eyes of the Lord.

If it's not scriptural, it's not right! With that being the case, the believer who has failed must not yield to such foolishness.

To do so will have a serious, adverse, spiritual effect upon him and could even cause him to lose his soul.

The curse of the modern church is rules made up by men who have no scriptural authority. The men are wrong to make up such rules, and men are wrong who obey such rules.

THE WOMAN

"And the LORD God said unto the woman, What is this that you have done? And the woman said, The serpent beguiled me, and I did eat" (Gen. 3:13).

"And the LORD God said unto the woman," presents the Lord, at least at the moment, not responding to Adam but now turning to the woman. We will find that her answer was far nobler than that of Adam, but yet, she still did not properly repent. She actually cast aspersion on the serpent.

THE QUESTION

By asking the question, *"What is this that you have done?"* the Lord placed the emphasis on the pronoun *you*.

Of course, God readily knew what Eve had done, why she did it, how she did it, and all about what had happened. In fact, that was not the point of the question.

Probably the two questions, *"Where are you?"* and *"What is this that you have done?"* comprise the human problem.

The Lord continues to ask the human race, *"Where are you?"* This implies, as previously stated, a place of trouble, difficulties, guilt, and bondage. However, that place and position were not arrived at without culpability on our part. It is because we have done something wrong! In effect, we have sinned against God, which has put us in this place of distress.

As we consider the horror that took place on Sept. 11, 2001, to be sure, these same questions are being asked by God to the entirety of America: *"Where are you?"* and *"What have you done?"*

In other words, even though we don't like to admit it, there is a cause.

The Lord does not steal, kill, and destroy. That is the work of Satan. In fact, Jesus said, *"I am come that they might have life, and that they might have it more abundantly"* (Jn. 10:10).

What happened in New York City, Washington, D.C., and the crashing of the airliner in Pennsylvania, were all caused by Satan. He is the one who steals, kills, and destroys (Jn. 10:10). Yet the Lord did have to allow the Evil One to do this thing, and with that being the case, why would He have allowed such? (Job, Chpts. 1–2).

As America now looks at herself, the Lord would ask the same question that He asked Adam: *"Where are you?"*

We would have to answer that we are in a mess, so to speak! Our economy has been hit hard; our vulnerability is now exposed to the entirety of the world; and our institutions are under attack. We find ourselves in a position with tens of thousands, and possibly even hundreds of thousands—grief-stricken, brokenhearted, and hurting because of the loss of loved ones.

THE RELIGION OF ISLAM

And now, our leaders, reaching all the way back to President Bill Clinton and even President George H. W. Bush, don't seem to understand the religion of Islam. They have adopted a policy that is totally wrong. They advocate that the far greater majority of Muslims are peace-loving people, with only a small percentage being radical.

They could not be more wrong!

The Muslims, and that includes all of them, hate us with a passion. If they had the power to do so, they would totally and completely murder this nation, literally murdering millions of people, and doing so without any qualms whatsoever. Our State Department is shot through with Muslims bent on destroying this country.

Under President Obama, the situation greatly increased instead of diminished. In fact, this man bitterly opposed the American way of life and would have liked to seen it turned over to Islam. As well, he hated Israel and did everything he could to weaken this sovereign state. He weakened our military until it is only a shadow of what it once was. This was done intentionally.

There is only one answer for America, and that is God. The Scripture still says the following: *"If My people, who are called by My name, shall humble themselves, and pray, and seek My face, and turn from their wicked ways; then will I hear from heaven, and will forgive their sin, and will heal their land"* (II Chron. 7:14).

MY PEOPLE

I pray there are enough true believers in the land to turn the tide. Let us say it again: It's because God is our only hope. If there is not a move of God of some sort, the America that we know today, and untold millions have known previously, will be no more. That's how critical the situation actually is. Powerful forces in this nation are trying to take God out of everything. It's no longer the separation of church and state, which is biblical, but rather a separation of God and state. In other words, great attempts are being made to erase every semblance of God, and especially Jesus Christ, completely out of every fabric of our society. This includes education, commerce, and the military, in other words, anything and everything that resembles the Word of God. The situation is far, far worse than anyone realizes.

When we embrace any part of the religion of Islam, we are embracing the most evil, the most ungodly, the most reprobate, and the most murderous religion or philosophy the world has ever known. It makes Genghis Khan look like a Sunday school picnic. In fact, it makes communism look tame by comparison.

I believe the answer to our dilemma is II Chronicles 7:14 alone. With that being done, He has plainly said that He will forgive our sin and will heal our land.

THE SERPENT

"And the woman said, The serpent beguiled me, and I did eat." In a sense Eve was blaming God, as well, simply

because God had made the serpent. So, in effect, she was saying, "Lord, if You hadn't made the serpent, I wouldn't be in this predicament!"

Did Satan through the serpent beguile and deceive Eve? Yes, he did! In fact, Satan is still the great deceiver (II Cor. 4:4). However, we should realize that God did not accept this excuse, as Verse 16 will show.

When she said, *"And I did eat,"* she was in actuality saying, "It's true that I did eat, but it was not my fault."

THE LORD GOD

"And the LORD God said unto the serpent, Because you have done this, you are cursed above all cattle, and above every beast of the field; upon your belly shall you go, and dust shall you eat all the days of your life" (Gen. 3:14).

When the Lord spoke to the serpent, He presented no question, and no interrogation was posed toward the serpent at all. God judged him, and it was in listening to this judgment that the guilty pair heard the first great promise respecting Christ.

THE CURSE

The phrase, *"Because you have done this, you are cursed above all cattle, and above every beast of the field,"* refers to this animal being reduced from possibly the highest place and position in the animal kingdom to the lowest. The very fact that the Lord leveled a curse at this creature lets us know that the animal must have had some intelligence, a limited power of choice, and even the power of limited speech.

The reptile, not being a moral creature, could not be cursed in the sense of being made susceptible to misery. However, it could be cursed in the sense of being deteriorated in its nature, and as it were, consigned to a lower position in the scale of being, which it was.

THE EXTENT OF THE CURSE

The statement, *"Upon your belly shall you go, and dust shall you eat all the days of your life,"* which was made by the Lord against the serpent, evidently means that it had previously functioned erect. With that being the case, it would have possessed a backbone, which would have given it the capability of standing upright, etc. The curse changed its skeletal framework.

The eating of dust is not meant to be taken literally, but it means that because of it crawling on its belly, its mouth is where the dust is, which refers to its inferior position.

ENMITY

"And I will put enmity between you and the woman, and between your seed and her seed; it shall bruise your head, and you shall bruise His heel" (Gen. 3:15).

The Lord now actually spoke to Satan, who had used the serpent.

Putting *"enmity between you* (Satan) *and the woman,"* in effect, says, "Use the woman to bring down the human race, and I will use the woman as an instrument to bring the Redeemer into the world, who will save the human race."

There will be enmity between *"her seed,"* who is the Lord Jesus Christ, and *"your seed,"* which pertains to those who follow Satan and includes almost the entirety of the human race.

Jesus, the seed of the woman, would bruise the head of the serpent on the Cross. The serpent would bruise the heel of the Saviour, which speaks of the suffering of the crucifixion.

MARY

Let us say it again: as Satan used the woman to bring sin into the world, the Lord would use the woman to bring the Redeemer into the world, who would save from sin.

However, in all of this, we are not to think that the Virgin Mary crushed the power of the Devil by giving birth to Christ. While she definitely was greatly honored by the Lord in being able to serve in this capacity, the truth is, Mary only provided a house, so to speak, for the birth of the Redeemer into this world. It is the Lord Jesus Christ, and the Lord Jesus Christ alone, who has redeemed us, and He did so by the giving of Himself on the Cross in the pouring out of His precious blood (Eph. 2:13–18).

In fact, Jesus had no similarities to His brothers and sisters simply because Joseph was not actually His father, and Mary only provided for Him a house, so to speak, for some nine months until He was born.

While we certainly hold Mary in high regard, it is, in fact, an abomination that the Catholic Church has attempted to make her a co-redemptress. Such thinking and Mary-worship can be construed as none other than blasphemy.

HER SEED

"And between your seed and her seed" refers to those who follow Satan (your seed) and to those who follow Christ (her seed).

In fact, this *"enmity,"* which refers to hatred, is played out in graphic detail in Chapter 4 of the book of Genesis, referring to Cain and his brother Abel, whom he murdered.

This enmity, or animosity, is prevalent between the unredeemed and the redeemed. It shows in the religions of the world that oppose Christ, and the more wicked these religions, the more opposition to Christ. In fact, the religion of Islam is the greatest example of all. It is without a doubt the wickedest religion in the world; consequently, it hates Christ, and with a venom one might quickly add.

Islam hates Israel simply because the Bible proclaims the truth that Isaac was the one through whom the Redeemer would come (Gen. 21:12). As well, the land of Israel was promised to Abraham's seed, who is Isaac (Gen. 28:13). The Muslims claim that Ishmael is Abraham's seed and that the land of Israel belongs to them.

MUHAMMAD

Muhammad, as are all Arabs, was a descendant of Ishmael. This conflict is the reason for the constant war of the Muslim world against Israel and their hatred for the United States. They hate Israel, and they hate the Lord Jesus Christ. Inasmuch as the Muslims look at America as the greatest citadel of Christianity, they refer to us as the "great Satan."

Some have tried to claim that Islam is a religion of love and a religion of peace. Nothing could be further from the truth. It is a religion of hate and a religion of war and violence. In fact, if Islam had its way, and if it had the power to do so, there would be no United States of America. They would blot it off the face of the earth, with every street in America running red with blood. That they don't do so is not for a lack of the will, but rather a lack of power.

However, this enmity doesn't stop with those who do not confess Christ versus those who do. It extends greatly to the church, as proven in this last phrase.

THE CROSS OF CHRIST

The phrase, *"It* (Christ) *shall bruise your head, and you shall bruise His heel,"* refers to what Christ would do to Satan through His death on the Cross and the sufferings of Christ that this would entail.

How exactly did Christ bruise the head of Satan on the Cross?

To bruise means to crush or trample down. A serpent bites. If his head is crushed, he can hardly continue to bite. This all speaks of what Jesus would accomplish on the Cross.

As God judged the serpent, it was in listening to this judgment that the guilty pair, Adam and Eve, heard the first great promise respecting Christ. We have here the sum of the whole matter, and the rest of the Bible explains the nature of this struggle, the persons who wage it, and the manner and consequences of the victory.

In this struggle, man is finally to prevail, but not unscathed. His triumph is to be gained not by mere human strength, but by the coming of one who is the woman's seed. Around this promised deliverer, the rest of Scripture groups itself. Leave out these words given in this verse, and all the inspired teaching that follows would be an ever-widening river without a fountainhead. Of necessity, with the fall came the promise of restoration. Grace was no afterthought but entered the world side by side with sin.

Upon this foundation, the rest of Holy Scripture is built till revelation at last reaches its cornerstone in Christ.

The enmity mentioned here has its greatest force in religion rather than in anything else. If it is to be noticed, the whole world is religious in one way or the other. Man was created to worship, in reality, to worship God. Consequently, even those who do not know God (who make up the majority of this world) actually worship something, whether the idol of religion or the idol of themselves.

However, in the ranks of Christianity, perhaps one can say this enmity is greater than ever. What do we mean by that?

To cut straight through, let us say immediately that the Cross of Christ is the dividing line of which we here speak. The last phrase of Verse 15 proclaims the Cross of Christ as the manner in which the head of Satan would be bruised. Now let us answer our question as to how it was bruised.

THE BRUISING OF THE HEAD OF SATAN

Let not the reader think that Jesus has fought Satan in some type of physical combat. To be sure, Satan wants no part of Christ. So, how did Jesus bruise the head of the serpent?

Paul tells us how: *"Blotting out the handwriting of ordinances that was against us, which was contrary to us, and took it out of the way, nailing it to His Cross; And having spoiled principalities and powers, He made a show of them openly, triumphing over them in it"* (Col. 2:14–15).

Jesus went to the Cross to satisfy the demands of a thrice-holy God. Man owed a terrible debt to God, which was brought on by sin—a debt, incidentally, that he could not even hope to pay. This debt was made very clear and plain by the law of Moses. In other words, the law told man what he should do and how he should be. Regrettably, due to man's fallen state, he could not live up to this which God demanded and was, therefore, branded by his own actions as a lawbreaker. The penalty for the breaking of this law was death (Rom. 6:23).

So, Jesus went to the Cross in order to pay that debt, which He did by the pouring out of His own precious blood (Eph. 2:13–18). This satisfied the demands of the righteousness of God, which means that the debt was paid in full. Jesus Christ was our substitute and, actually, our representative man (I Cor. 15:45). Simple faith in Him grants to us a perfect and complete salvation. At the moment of faith, a perfect righteousness is imputed to the believing sinner, and he is born again (Jn. 3:3, 16; Eph. 2:8–9).

SIN

However, as a by-product of what Jesus did at the Cross, Satan was totally and completely defeated. His head was forever bruised, which means that the terrible bite of sin and death was made invalid. So, what was that by-product?

Sin is Satan's legal claim on humanity. By the word *legal,* we are referring to the right that Satan has to hold man in bondage because of sin.

In fact, this bondage was so complete that all Old Testament saints were taken captive by Satan at death and taken down into paradise. Because of their faith, Satan couldn't put them over into the burning side of the pit, but he definitely was holding them captive (Lk., Chpt. 16).

However, when Jesus died on the Cross, thereby, paying the sin debt, Satan's legal right was canceled. In that manner, Jesus bruised the head of Satan, which means that He spoiled principalities and powers, making a show of them openly, triumphing over them in it (Col. 2:15).

In fact, the moment that Jesus died on the Cross, He immediately went down into paradise, where Paul said, *"He led captivity captive, and gave gifts unto men"* (Eph. 4:8).

HE LED CAPTIVITY CAPTIVE

"He led captivity captive" is a strange term. It means that all the Old Testament saints, as stated, were held captive by Satan when they died. This means that they couldn't go to heaven but were rather taken down into paradise, as also stated. We must remember that paradise was only separated from the burning side of hell by a great gulf (Lk. 16:26). This means that they couldn't go to heaven because the sin debt remained.

However, when Jesus paid the price, thereby, removing the sin debt, this destroyed Satan's power of captivity, with Jesus then making them His captives, which He did. As well, he took them with Him to heaven. From that moment, whenever believers die, they immediately go to be with Christ (Phil. 1:23).

While believers were definitely saved before the Cross because of their faith in the coming Redeemer, the truth was, the blood of bulls and goats couldn't take away sins (Heb. 10:4). However, when Jesus came, He was introduced by John the Baptist—that great prophet who said of Him, *"Behold the Lamb of God, which takes away the sin of the world"* (Jn. 1:29).

If it is to be noticed, John used the word *sin* in a singular sense, while Paul used it in Hebrews 10:4 in a plural sense (sins). What is the difference?

Animal sacrifices had to be offered up for each sin, hence, the word *sins* being used. Even though the animal sacrifices covered the sin, thus, the word *atonement* being used often in the Old Testament, it still couldn't take away these sins.

THE FINISHED WORK OF CHRIST

However, when Jesus came, He definitely addressed *sins* in the plural, which speaks of every single sin that anyone has ever committed being washed and cleansed, at least for those who will accept Him as Saviour. He, as well, addressed the very cause and principle of sin, hence, John the Baptist using the term in the singular. In other words, Jesus took away the cause of sin, which is Satan and self-will. When He bruised the head of Satan on the Cross, which He did by paying the debt for all sin, it went to the very cause and principle of sin.

Let the reader understand that this was all done at the Cross. This is why it is called *the finished work* (Jn. 17:4; 19:30). God using the metaphor regarding the heel being bruised refers to Jesus suffering on the Cross. In other words, the bruising of the head of Satan didn't come without price. It cost our Lord His very life; however, due to the fact that He atoned for every sin, the resurrection was never in doubt. In other words, because the wages of sin is death, had He left one sin unatoned, He couldn't have been resurrected from the dead. However, due to the fact that He definitely did atone for all sin, there was no way that death could hold Him. The resurrection was a foregone conclusion.

THE SHEDDING OF THE BLOOD OF CHRIST

That's the reason that at the moment of His death, the Scripture says: *"Behold, the veil of the temple was rent in twain from the top to the bottom"* (Mat. 27:51).

This means that the way into the Holy of Holies, the very presence of God, was now opened to man. Jesus had opened it by what He did at the Cross. At that moment, the plan of redemption was complete.

Yes, there had to be a resurrection; however, as stated, the resurrection was never in doubt! It was the shedding of His blood on the Cross that paid the terrible sin debt and, thereby, opened up the way to the presence of God, and this great work was totally and completely finished at the Cross. It did not await the resurrection or the exaltation. While those things were definitely necessary, as stated, due to the price being paid at the Cross and God having recognized that sacrifice by ripping the veil apart, the resurrection and the exaltation were a guaranteed fact.

When Christians boast about being a resurrection person, they need to understand that they are such only by what Christ did at the Cross. Paul said, *"For if we have been planted together in the likeness of His death, we shall be also in the likeness of His resurrection"* (Rom. 6:5).

This simply means that we cannot enjoy resurrection power, which I will explain momentarily, unless we first understand *"the likeness of His death,"* which refers to our part in that death, as outlined in Romans 6:3–5.

THE CROSS AS THE DIVIDING LINE

This enmity of which the Lord spoke becomes even more rabid in the church of the Lord Jesus Christ. Satan tells the world that they can have salvation without Jesus Christ and Him crucified. He brings that lie over into the church by telling believers that they can have victory other than by Jesus Christ and Him crucified. This is where the Cross is the dividing line.

If the believer rejects the Cross as it regards the means of not only his salvation but, as well, his sanctification, he will grow leaner and leaner in his soul, with even the potential of losing his soul. Paul said so in Galatians, Chapter 5. If he accepts the Message of the Cross and looks strictly to what Jesus did at Calvary as the means of his life of victory and sanctification, he will grow in grace and the knowledge of the Lord. The fruit of the Spirit will then be paramount within his life (Gal. 5:22–23). Otherwise, the works of the flesh will manifest themselves in his life (Gal. 5:19–21).

WORKS OF THE FLESH OR FRUIT OF THE SPIRIT?

So, the believer has a choice between the following:

- Works of the flesh

- Fruit of the Spirit

The latter comes by faith in the Cross, with the former coming by faith in self. Now, the upshot is this: Most of the time, those in the church who reject the Cross will at the same time persecute those who accept the Cross. Again, Paul said so: *"And I, brethren, if I yet preach circumcision, why do I yet suffer persecution? then is the offence of the Cross ceased"* (Gal. 5:11).

The Cross has always been the dividing line between the true church and the apostate church. It is because the Cross of Christ is the foundation of the gospel exactly as the Lord says in the verse of our study, Genesis 3:15.

THE WOMAN

"Unto the woman He said, I will greatly multiply your sorrow and your conception; in sorrow you shall bring forth children; and your desire shall be to your husband, and he shall rule over you." (Gen. 3:16).

This presents judgment that was bitter to say the least, which, as well, had to do with the fall. In other words, it had far-reaching effects.

We find that the Lord now spoke to the woman as it regarded her judgment. He would multiply her sorrow. Her conception of children would no longer be as sons of God (Lk. 3:38), but rather as sons, or in the likeness, of Adam (Gen. 5:3).

Children would be born into a world of sorrow. Her husband, instead of God, would now rule over her.

And yet, even though the Lord placed a curse upon the serpent, He did not do so as it regarded Adam and Eve, at least as it regarded them personally. This referred to the fact that human beings are candidates for restoration.

CONCEPTION

The phrase, *"I will greatly multiply your sorrow and your conception,"* carries forth the idea that with the fall of Adam, all of humanity, in essence, fell because all were in his loins (I Cor. 15:21–22).

Adam was the fountainhead of the human race. What he was, all would be. That's the reason that in order for man to be redeemed, there would have to be another Adam sent into this world, whom Paul referred to as the *"last Adam,"* who was the Lord Jesus Christ (I Cor. 15:45).

The word *conception* is used here, and the multiplying of sorrow was simply because children were originally intended by God to be brought into the world literally as sons of God (Lk. 3:38).

Instead, due to the fall, all children would be conceived in sorrow, referring to the fact that they would be brought into the world in the likeness of Adam with his fallen nature (Gen. 5:3). As a result of this fallen nature, i.e., the sin nature, man's every bent and direction would be toward sin, hence, all the pain, suffering, privation, poverty, want, death, dying, and war.

CHILDREN

The phrase, *"In sorrow you shall bring forth children,"* refers to what we have just said. How many mothers have wept bitter tears because their sons and daughters have turned out to be murderers, thieves, etc.? How many have had their hearts broken by the actions of their children? While Christ has made it possible for all of this to be ameliorated, without Him, to be sure, the sorrow prevails.

RULE

The phrase, *"And your desire shall be to your husband, and he shall rule over you,"* pertains to the fact that because of Eve being the prime actor in sin, henceforward, she was to live in subjection to Adam.

Among the heathen, the punishment was made very bitter by the degradation to which a woman was reduced. In fact, this continues unto this hour in the ranks of Islam.

As Paul teaches, thankfully, in Christ, the whole penalty has been abrogated (Gal. 3:28), and the Christian woman is no more inferior to the man than is the Gentile to the Jew or the bondman to the free. This was made possible by what Jesus did at the Cross. There, He totally and completely liberated mankind, which, of course, included all women. So, every iota of freedom that a woman presently possesses, which should be totally and completely equal to that of the man, is owed completely to Christ and what He did for us at the Cross.

Prior to the fall, woman was the helpmate of her husband and his equal. After the fall, she was no longer his equal, but now in Christ, she has been restored to that previous position of equality.

In the marriage relationship, the husband is to love the wife as Christ loved the church and gave Himself for it (Eph. 5:25), and the wife is to respect the leadership of the husband.

ADAM

"And unto Adam He said, Because you have hearkened unto the

voice of your wife, and have eaten of the tree, of which I commanded you, saying, You shall not eat of it: cursed is the ground for your sake; in sorrow shall you eat of it all the days of your life" (Gen. 3:17).

The phrase, *"And unto Adam He said, Because you have hearkened unto the voice of your wife,"* proclaims the fact that Adam didn't listen to God.

Adam hearkened unto his wife instead of God. As his penalty, the ground was to be cursed, meaning that there would be no more garden of Eden.

Instead of God feeding him, he would have to derive his nourishment from a cursed ground. Consequently, his life would be that of sorrow.

Eve is representative here of people who tend to be used by Satan to draw others away from the Word of God. Man can listen to man, or man can listen to God. He cannot listen to both! The tragedy is that most in the world are listening to men instead of God. In fact, in I Timothy 2:14, the Holy Spirit teaches that Adam sinned more deeply than his wife. She is condemned in Genesis 3:16 to subjection to him; prior to that condemnation, she was his helpmate or equal.

THE TREE

The phrase, *"And have eaten of the tree, of which I commanded you, saying, You shall not eat of it,"* speaks of the Tree of the Knowledge of Good and Evil as portrayed in Genesis 2:17.

As we have previously stated, the problem with the tree in question was not evil properties in the fruit, but rather disobedience to the Word of God. Because this is so very, very important, please allow us to say it again.

OBEDIENCE

Obedience to the Word of God is the criterion for all things. I think any true Christian would readily agree with that statement; however, the great question pertains to the *how* of obedience. In other words, we are commanded to obey, and every true Christian wants to obey, but the question is how do we bring this about?

Regrettably, the answer to this question that would be given by most Christians would be that we just simply obey. Most Christians have the idea that now that we are Christians, we have the capacity to say yes or no with ease; consequently, if we say yes to sin and temptation, it is simply because we want to do that. Nothing could be further from the truth. To be frank, millions of Christians have run aground on this very premise.

THE HATRED OF SIN

If that is the case, then why did the great apostle Paul say, *"For that which I do I allow* (understand) *not: for what I would, that do I not; but what I hate, that do I"* (Rom. 7:15). I have asked that in the form of a question, even though I ended it with a period.

Some try to explain away the entirety of Chapter 7 of Romans by claiming that this is an account of Paul's experiences before salvation. Nothing could be further from the truth.

In the first place, Paul says here that he hates sin. No sinner or unredeemed person hates sin. He may hate the effects of sin, but he certainly doesn't hate sin. In fact, he loves sin.

No, Chapter 7 of Romans, which is, incidentally, one of the most important chapters in the entirety of the Bible, proclaims the experience of the apostle Paul after he was saved and baptized with the Holy Spirit. In fact, he had already been called to be an apostle, and even then was an apostle.

His problem was this: At that time, and I speak of the time of the Romans, Chapter 7, experience, Paul didn't know the Message of the Cross.

In fact, no one else in the world knew that particular message either. Actually, this message was given to the apostle Paul, which, in reality, is the meaning of the new covenant, which is the meaning of the Cross.

WILLPOWER

Paul is relating his experiences of trying to live for God by his own strength and ability, which are always woefully insufficient, but the tragedy is, that's where most Christians are presently—in Chapter 7 of Romans.

In Verse 18 of that chapter, the apostle says, *"For I know that in me (that is, in my flesh,) dwells no good thing: for to will (willpower) is present with me; but how to perform that which is good I find not."*

He is plainly saying in this passage that willpower within itself, which simply refers to saying yes or no, will not suffice.

But yet, that's what most Christians find themselves doing. They're trying to obey the Lord by saying yes to Him and no to temptation. Sooner or later, they fail!

GOD'S WAY

There's only one way that the believer can obey the Lord, which refers to obeying God's Word. That way is as follows:

- We must understand that everything from God comes to us strictly through what Jesus did at the Cross. It's not our willpower, our own personal strength or ability, or any machinations in which we may engage, but strictly the Cross of Christ. There, every victory was won (Rom. 6:1-14; I Cor. 1:17-18, 23; 2:2).

- Understanding that, the Cross of Christ is to ever be the object of our faith. This means that if the Cross of Christ is the total and complete object of our faith, which it must be, then our own ability and strength, our church, or whatever, is not the object of our faith. This is very, very important (Gal. 6:14; Col. 2:10-15).

- With the understanding that the Cross is the means by which all things come to the child of God, and that it must ever be the object of our faith, the Holy Spirit will then greatly and grandly help us in all things (Rom. 8:1–11; Eph. 2:13-18).

Now, the reader will find that in one way or the other, I will give this little abbreviated formula over and over again throughout this volume. I do so because there is nothing more important.

This is the manner and, in fact, the only manner in which the believer can properly obey the Word of the Lord. If we set out to do it any other way, we will find ourselves, whether we admit it or not, in the position of Paul when he said, *"O wretched man that I am! Who shall deliver me from the body of this death?"* (Rom. 7:24).

THE CURSE

The phrase, *"Cursed is the ground for your sake; in sorrow shall you eat of it all the days of your life,"* presents the cursing of the habitation. What the earth would have been, in fact, was intended to be, which was a paradise, has now been altered, and altered severely.

As well, the phrase, *"All the days of your life,"* proclaims the death sentence, which means that life is now terminal, all as a result of spiritual death, which was and is separation from God.

As well, as sorrow was to be the end result of the children conceived and brought forth, likewise, sorrow would be the result of one's labor.

Matthew Henry said: "Man's business shall from henceforth become a toil to him. Observe here that labor is our duty, which we must faithfully perform; not as creatures only, but as criminals, we are bound to work; it is a part of our sentence, which idleness daringly defies. Uneasiness and weariness with labor are our just punishment, which we must patiently submit to, and not complain of, since they are less than our iniquity deserves."[7]

Henry went on to say, "Let us not by inordinate care and labor make our punishment heavier than God has made it; but study to lighten our burden, by regarding providence in all, and expecting rest shortly."[8]

The righteousness of God is to be acknowledged in all the sad consequences of sin. Yet, in God's sentence, there is mercy. Man is not sentenced to eat dust as the serpent, but only to eat the herb of the field.

THORNS AND THISTLES

"Thorns also and thistles shall it bring forth to you; and you shall eat the herb of the field" (Gen. 3:18).

Thorns and thistles were not originally in the creation of God. Such are the result of the curse, which is a result of the sin of man.

The herb of the field would not now grow freely, as originally intended, but only now with great care and labor.

Verse 18 proclaims the fact that left to itself, the ground will no longer bring forth choice trees laden with generous fruit, such as Adam found in the garden, but will now rather bring forth thorns and thistles.

The tendency of the earth is now toward decay and degeneration, again, all because of the curse. In the renewed earth, the golden age of paradise (we speak of the coming kingdom age) will return, meaning that the curse will then be lifted.

HERB OF THE FIELD

"And you shall eat the herb of the field." (Gen. 3:18).

Even with modern equipment, the produce of the earth is brought forth only with great care and diligence. Even then, it is prone to destruction regarding the elements, insects, etc. We can thank original sin for that.

If it is to be noticed, I think one could also say without fear of contradiction that it is the nations of the world that embrace Christianity, or at least a modicum of Christianity, that serve as the breadbaskets of the world. Nations that do not recognize Jesus as Lord can little feed their people, much less help feed others. One might say, "Much Bible, much food; little Bible, little food; no Bible, no food."

SWEAT

"In the sweat of your face shall you eat bread, till you return unto the ground; for out of it were you taken: for dust you are, and unto dust shall you return" (Gen. 3:19).

Man would find that food would now be obtained by hard labor. The life-source, which was formerly in God, is now in food, which is woefully insufficient. Physical death is the result.

The power of God alone could keep the dust alive; with that being gone, to dust man returns.

The phrase, *"In the sweat of your face shall you eat bread,"* proclaims the fact of hard labor as it regards the producing of food. As well, it presents itself as proof (and we continue to speak of sweat) that man is returning to the earth. It tells of exhaustion and waste.

Toil is the lot of the human race, which, as stated, God never originally intended.

DUST

"Till you return unto the ground; for out of it were you taken: for dust you are, and unto dust shall you return."

To prove the immortality of the soul equally proves the mortality of the body.

Bishop Butler says:

Death is the division of a compound substance in its component parts; but as the soul is a simple substance and incapable of division, it is per se incapable of death. The body of Adam, composed of particles of earth, was capable of division, and our first parents in Paradise were assured of an unending existence by a special gift, typified by the tree of life. But now this gift was withdrawn, and henceforward the sweat of man's brow was in itself proof that he was returning to the earth.[9]

ADAM AND CHRIST

In one way or the other, men constantly claim that the sentence passed upon Adam was too harsh (too severe). As is usual, man continues to blame God for his dilemma. Even after some 6,000 years of recorded history, he refuses to acknowledge the blame as being his own.

To be sure, the situation is made worse by man ignoring the fact that sin demanded such a sentence, and above all, that Jesus answered that sentence by becoming the last Adam, which wrought redemption for man.

Note the following:

- Travailing pain came with sin. We read of the travail of Christ's soul, even though He had no sin (Isa. 53:11), and the pains of death that He suffered (Acts 2:24).

- Subjection came with sin. In answer to this, Christ was made under the law (Gal. 4:4).

- The curse came with sin. In answer to that horror, Christ was made a curse for us and, in effect, died a cursed death (Gal. 3:13).

- The thorns came in with sin. In answer to that, Jesus was crowned with thorns for us.

- Sweat, as well, came in with sin. The Scripture says of Him that His sweat for us was as it had been great drops of blood.

- Sorrow came with sin. He was a man of sorrows, acquainted with grief.

- Death came with sin. He became obedient unto death. Thus is the cure as wide as the cause.

MATTHEW HENRY

Concerning the fall, Matthew Henry said: "Man's soul was ruined by the fall; the image of God was defaced; man's nature was corrupted, and he became dead in sin. The design of God was to restore the soul of man; to restore life, and the image of God, in conversion; and to carry on this work in sanctification, until He should perfect it in glory."[10]

One must also say that man's body was ruined by the fall when it became subject to death. The design of God was to restore it from this ruin. His plan was not only to deliver it from death by what He did at the Cross through His Son, the Lord Jesus Christ, but to deliver it, as well, from mortality itself in making it like unto Christ's glorious body (I Jn. 3:2).

EVE

"And Adam called his wife's name Eve; because she was the mother of all living" (Gen. 3:20).

The name *Eve* actually means "life" or "the mother of all the living." The idea is that through Eve alone could human life be continued and the woman's seed be obtained, who was to raise up man from his fall. While woman's punishment consists in the multiplication of her sorrow and conception, she becomes, thereby, only more precious to man.

And yet, Eve did not fully understand what the Lord had said concerning the seed of the woman. In fact, it would not be fully brought out until the prophet Isaiah gave clarity to the promise by saying, *"Behold, a virgin shall conceive"* (Isa. 7:14). This prophecy made it clear that the Saviour was not to be the offspring of the union of a man and wife. In the New Testament, this fact was revealed still more clearly by the angel (Lk. 1:26–38).

Since then, there was promised man, through the seed of the woman, deliverance from the law, sin, and death. There was given to him a clear and sure hope of the resurrection and renewal in the future life. It is clear that he could not remove sin and its punishment by his own power, and neither could he escape death and make amends for his disobedience by his own power. Therefore, the Son of God had to sacrifice Himself and secure all of this for mankind. He had to remove sin, overcome death, and restore what Adam had lost by his disobedience.

MOTHER OF ALL LIVING

The phrase, *"Because she was the mother of all living,"* proclaims the power of procreation. But yet, some believe that in Adam giving the name Eve to his wife, it pertains to the proclamation of his faith. That is possible, but I think not!

Faith in the promised seed was the requirement for salvation. There is some evidence, which we will later explore more fully, that Adam and Eve may have made a start toward God. In other words, they may have initially expressed faith; however, every evidence is that they soon abandoned their faith.

The Scripture tells us of the faith of Enoch, who was contemporary with Adam, at least for a period of time, but it says nothing about the faith of Adam (Heb. 11:5–6).

COATS OF SKINS

"Unto Adam also and to his wife did the LORD God make coats of skins, and clothed them" (Gen. 3:21).

In the making of coats of skins, God, in effect, was telling Adam and Eve that their fig leaves were insufficient.

From this, it seems that Adam in some way, even immediately after the fall, must have been taught that without shedding of blood, there was no remission of sin, and that God would accept a vicarious (substitutionary) sacrifice.

In this first sacrifice was laid the foundation of the entire Mosaic dispensation—that of the gospel—as in Verse 15.

It is important that the promise of the gospel, which is the sacrifice of Christ, was given first (Vs. 15), while that which represented Moses was given second. The Mosaic law would be temporary, always pointing to Christ who would be the great sacrifice.

The animals that the Lord had to kill, in essence, were a sacrifice, or Christ in a figure, who is, therefore, said to be the Lamb slain from the foundation of the world (I Pet. 1:18-20).

Let it be known that it is the Lord God who furnished these coats and not man himself. This tells us that salvation is altogether of God and not at all of man. All Adam and Eve could do was fashion a garment out of fig leaves, which, regrettably, man has been attempting to do ever since.

Sin is not a cheap affair and cannot be satisfied by a cheap solution. Sin is devastating and can only be addressed by the sacrifice of Christ, which was, incidentally, the ultimate sacrifice.

FROM THE VERY BEGINNING, THE CROSS!

The manner in which the Lord would redeem the human race has never been in question. In fact, that was decided by the Godhead even before the foundation of the world (I Pet. 1:18–20).

Someone asked me once, "Was it who Christ was, or what He did that effected our salvation?"

Up front, it was both—who He was *and* what He did!

While who He was, namely deity, was absolutely necessary, still, Jesus Christ, in fact, had always been God. As God, He had no beginning, which means that He was unformed, unmade, uncreated, has always been, always is, and always shall be. However, none of that, as wonderful and glorious as it was and is, redeemed anybody. In fact, His virgin birth did not redeem anyone, and neither did His miracles or healings! The fact that He spoke as no man ever spoke did not effect any redemption, even though all of these things were of extreme significance.

THE CROSS

It was what He did on the Cross that effected redemption. That's why Paul said, *"For Christ sent me not to baptize, but to preach the gospel: not with wisdom of words, lest the Cross of Christ should be made of none effect"* (I Cor. 1:17).

As well, when we're given a vision of heaven through the eyes of John the Beloved (I speak of his great vision on the Isle of Patmos), we see there the central theme is Jesus Christ and Him crucified. This is signified by the apostle's constant use of the term *"Lamb"* (Rev. 5:6, 8, 12–13).

So, it begins with the Cross, and it ends with the Cross. In fact, John used the term *"Lamb,"* signifying Christ and what He did at the Cross, some 28 times in the book of Revelation, and seven times in the last two chapters alone.

The last time in the Bible the term *"Lamb"* is used (we continue to speak of the Son of God), it is used in relationship to the fact that there is *"no more curse"* (Rev. 22:3). In other words, the terrible curse that was leveled at the dawn of time as it regarded Adam's fall, was eliminated by the Lord Jesus Christ at great price, which was the shedding of His life's blood on the Cross.

COVERING

The three words, *"and clothed them,"* proclaim the fact that such a covering came at a price—the death of the animals in question. Consequently, these coats of skin had a significance. The beasts, whose skins they were, had to be slain, and slain before their eyes, to show them what death is, and that they might see that they themselves were mortal and dying (Eccl. 3:18). As well, this sacrifice would also show them the terrible awfulness of sin. As repeatedly stated, it would typify the coming Redeemer.

Jesus said to the church at Laodicea, *"I counsel you to buy of Me gold tried in the fire, that you may be rich; and white raiment, that you may be clothed, and that the shame of your nakedness do not appear"* (Rev. 3:18).

The Laodiceans had abandoned the Cross. They were trusting in other things; consequently, the shame of their nakedness was obvious!

All of this becomes even more striking when we realize that the Laodicean church typifies the church of this present time. It is referred to as the apostatized church. Let the reader understand that the apostasy addressed here is the abandonment of the Cross.

In the last several decades, all types of things have been suggested as the proper covering. Many think of their denominations as their covering; others think of particular preachers; still others think of their own good works.

Irrespective of what it might be and how good it might seem to be on the surface, if the covering is not the blood of the Lamb, and that exclusively, then it is nothing but fig leaves. It is something that God will not honor, in fact, cannot honor, and that is the sin of the modern church.

THE CHURCH

While the church in its purest form belongs to Christ, with it actually being referred to as *"My church"* (Mat. 16:18), the sadness is, it is seldom left in its purest form.

Millions of so-called Christians have made a particular church the object of their faith. In other words, they think by their association and their involvement, such is their covering. They may not use that term, but the facts are, that particular church, whatever it might be, is their object of faith. They might talk about Christ and might even state that their trust is in Christ, but, in reality, it's in that church. In fact, many equate Christ and the church as somewhat one and the same. They aren't!

As a believer, your faith is to be anchored totally and completely in Christ. However, for it to actually be anchored in Christ, it must be defined by what He did at the Cross; otherwise, you are serving *"another Jesus"* (II Cor. 11:4).

THE CROSS

Millions claim to be serving Christ when, in reality, it is *"another Jesus"* that they are serving. Let me say it again, the reason is because of the following: To claim Jesus alone is not enough. One must claim what He did at the Cross as well! That's why Paul plainly said, *"But we preach Christ crucified"* (I Cor. 1:23).

He also said, *"For I determined not to know anything among you, save Jesus Christ, and Him crucified"* (I Cor. 2:2).

Satan doesn't really care too very much where one places one's faith as long as it's not in the Cross. He is perfectly content for you to place your faith in the greatest of Christian virtues. He knows that the Holy Spirit will not honor such an object of faith, which will leave the believer pretty well helpless. At that juncture, Satan can have his way with such a person. That's the reason for so many failures among Christians—failures, incidentally, which run the gamut all the way from the proverbial A to Z (I Cor. 1:17–18).

The covering has always been the Cross; the covering is presently the Cross; and the covering will ever be the Cross. There is no other.

TO KNOW GOOD AND EVIL

"And the LORD God said, Behold, the man is become as one of us, to know good and evil: and now, lest he put forth his hand, and take also of the Tree of Life, and eat, and live forever" (Gen. 3:22).

The phrase, *"And the LORD God said, Behold, the man is become as one of us, to know good and evil,"* refers to the Lord knowing evil by the power of omniscience, which knows all things, but never by personal experience. The Scripture says, *"For God cannot be tempted with evil"* (James 1:13).

This means that He cannot have anything to do with evil in any regard. He is perfectly righteous, actually, the thrice-holy God (Rev. 4:8).

As well, the pronoun "us" proclaims the Trinity. No, when the Lord used the pronoun "us," He wasn't speaking of Himself and angels, as suggested by some. As well, fallen angels know what evil is by personal experience, but not by omniscience, because no angel has that attribute. Such pertains only to deity.

THE TREE OF LIFE

The phrase, *"Lest he put forth his hand, and take also of the Tree of Life, and eat, and live forever,"* proclaims the fact that the fruit of this particular tree evidently contained certain properties designed by God that would cause the human body to remain forever young and, thereby, live forever. And yet, at the same time, we must be quick to say that this tree had such power not because of its peculiar nature, but because of the divine word attached to it, which made it a life-giving tree.

At the dawn of time, man was denied access to the Tree of Life, while at the conclusion of the dispensations, due to what Christ has done at the Cross, the Tree of Life is once again opened to man (Rev. 22:1–2).

EXPELLED FROM THE GARDEN OF EDEN

"Therefore the LORD *God sent him forth from the garden of Eden, to till the ground from whence he was taken"* (Gen. 3:23).

The Lord sending Adam and Eve away from the garden was, in fact, an act of mercy. Man is expelled from the garden lest by eating of the Tree of Life he should perpetuate his misery.

To bring this up to modern times, think of someone living forever who is like an Adolph Hitler, a Joseph Stalin, or the Muslims who murdered nearly 3,000 people by their acts of atrocity in New York City, Washington, D.C., and Pennsylvania!

In fact, that list is very long. While being driven from the garden of Eden and access to the Tree of Life was definitely a punishment, in the long run, because of their state, it was definitely a blessing, not only to them but to the entirety of the world.

Ellicott said:

> Adam had exercised the power of marring God's work, and if an unending physical life were added to the gift of freewill now in revolt against God, his condition and that of mankind would become most miserable. Man is still able to attain to immortality, but it must now be through struggle, sorrow, penitence, faith, and death. Hence a paradise is no fit home for him. The divine mercy, therefore, commands Adam to quit it, in order that he may live under conditions better suited for his moral and spiritual good.[11]

TILL THE GROUND

The phrase, *"To till the ground from whence he was taken,"* refers to a place of toil, not to a place of torment. Matthew Henry said, "Our first parents were excluded from the privileges of their state of innocency, yet they were not abandoned to despair."[12]

The word *till,* as used here, is the same Hebrew word rendered *dress* in Genesis 2:15. Adam's task is the same, but the conditions are now altered. In other words, it will now be far more difficult than was previously intended.

EXPULSION

"So He drove out the man; and He placed at the east of the garden of Eden cherubims, and a flaming sword which turned every way, to keep the way of the Tree of Life" (Gen. 3:24).

The word *drove* combined with the word *sent* in the previous verse imply that Adam and Eve definitely didn't want to depart paradise. Consequently, the two words *sent* and *drove* convey the ideas of "force and displeasure." In other words, God had to force Adam and Eve to leave.

However, there is one thing that all men must learn: Whatever God does with us is always and without exception for our best. In other words, if we did what we wanted to do, whatever that might be, to be sure, it would turn out to be destructive not only to others, but also to ourselves. To Adam and Eve, it seemed harsh to be driven out of the garden and not allowed access anymore. However, the plan of God was for their everlasting good, as well as all of humanity, because, in essence, what God did to our first parents was done to the entirety of the human race.

The idea was that they would look to the coming promised seed of Genesis 3:15. Had they partaken of the Tree of Life in their fallen state, such would have consigned them to an eternal life of torment, which would grow worse by the millennia. Only the promised seed could alleviate the dilemma! What does this teach us?

THE CROSS: THE ONLY ANSWER TO SIN

Out of the horror of Sept. 11, 2001, one man made the following observation: In looking at the rubble of the World Trade Center, in endeavoring to untangle the great steel beams so they could be hauled away, the workmen had fashioned a perfect cross with their cutting torches. That cross stood outlined against the wreckage. In looking at this, the man stated, "I wonder if the Lord is not trying to tell us something."

In fact, the Lord most definitely is trying to tell us something. He is telling us, in essence, that the cause of this terrible problem is sin, with the only solution to this problem being the Cross. There is no other answer for sin, no other answer for disobedience, and no other answer for rebellion. The Cross alone is the answer. Let the church understand that and let the preacher proclaim that. Let every believer understand that and let the world know that. The only answer is the Cross!

The idea is this: even though God was forced to drive Adam and Eve out of the garden, the sense of the text is that He went with them, which, in essence, said, "I will bring you back."

Oh, the love of God, how rich, how pure! Yes, He would bring man back but at such price, a price, incidentally, that He would pay Himself.

In 1997, in answer to years of soul-searching prayer, even with travail and tears, the Lord began to open up to me the Message of the Cross. To be sure, I had always preached the Cross and had done so strongly. As a result, the Lord had helped me to see hundreds of thousands brought to a saving knowledge of Jesus Christ, and I exaggerate not!

However, even though I knew and understood the Cross as it regarded the great salvation message, "Jesus died for me," I did not understand the Cross as it regarded the sanctification process. In other words, I didn't understand how we are to live for God, how we are to order our behavior, or how we are to have victory over the world, the flesh, and the Devil. Consequently, I attempted to sanctify myself, which cannot be done. God's righteousness is always set forth in the Cross. Man's righteousness is set forth in his own works—the sin-stained works—of his own hands. These are works that God cannot accept.

The closing verses of this chapter are full of instruction. Fallen man, in his fallen state, must not be allowed to eat of the fruit of the Tree of Life, for that would entail upon him endless wretchedness in this world. To take of the Tree of Life and eat and live forever in our present condition would be unmingled misery. To be sure, the Tree of Life can only be tasted in death and resurrection (I speak of our dying in Christ as it regards His crucifixion [Rom. 6:3]), and then being raised in *"newness of life"* (Rom. 6:4–5). This is the finished work of the promised seed, and it is by that and that alone that re-entry can be gained to the Tree of Life, who is the Lord Jesus Christ.

CHERUBIM

The phrase, *"And He placed at the east of the garden of Eden cherubims,"* evidently refers to the entrance to the garden.

There is some evidence, as we shall see, that a sanctuary was built there, and we continue to speak of the entrance to the garden, even as the next chapter in Genesis proclaims.

Who and what are these cherubim?

There are all types of opinions. Some say they are the fullness of the Deity. Some say the cherubim are symbolic of earthly life.

Others say they are of the angelic nature. Still others claim they represent the divine manhood of Jesus Christ.

Wordsworth says, "and I think he is right", "The cherubims are symbolic of redeemed and glorified humanity."[13]

He went on to say: "Combining with the intelligence of human nature the highest qualities of the animal world, as exhibited in the lion, the ox, and the eagle (Rev. 4:7), they were emblematic of creature life in its most absolute perfect form. As such they were caused to dwell at the gate of Eden to intimate that only when perfected and purified could fallen human nature return to Paradise."[14]

Carrying forth the same principle, the veil that hung between the Holy of Holies, where resided the ark of the covenant, and the Holy Place had cherubim embroidered on it (Ex. 26:31–32). In effect, the cherubim on the veil said the same thing as the cherubim at the entrance of the garden of Eden. Man was not allowed entrance. In fact, only the high priest of Israel could go into the Holy of Holies, and then only once a year, which was on the great Day of Atonement, and then not without blood.

BLOOD

In other words, he had to offer up the blood of the sacrifice, which was carried out at the brazen altar on the mercy seat that covered the ark of the covenant. This, as well, carried two cherubim, one on either end, facing each other and looking down upon the mercy seat. This high priest was a type of Christ, who would one day offer up His own blood on the Cross of

Calvary, which He did! That alone opened up the way to God, making it possible for man to come into the very presence of God. However, let it ever be known that this could be done, and can be done, only by our faith in the finished work of Christ.

The writer of Hebrews tells us, *"Let us* (believers) *therefore come boldly unto the throne of grace, that we may obtain mercy, and find grace to help in time of need"* (Heb. 4:16).

Let us say again that the way into paradise has now been opened by the Lord Jesus Christ, which He accomplished by the shedding of His own precious blood, which was effected at the Cross of Calvary. That's the reason that Paul said, *"For Christ sent me not to baptize, but to preach the gospel: not with wisdom of words, lest the Cross of Christ should be made of none effect"* (I Cor. 1:17).

THE FLAMING SWORD

The phrase, *"And a flaming sword which turned every way, to keep the way of the Tree of Life,"* tells us that this served as an emblem of the divine glory in its attitude toward sin.

"To keep the way of the Tree of Life," presents itself as an interesting statement. While it pertains to the way being kept shut, it also, at the same time, states that the way is to be kept open. In other words, the idea is, even as we've already stated, while God did drive Adam and Eve from the garden, He went with them, with a promise of bringing them (mankind) back. This was done by the *"promised seed,"* who is the Lord Jesus Christ, and who effected the open way by what He did at the Cross.

In effect, even as we will later study, the Lord showed to Jacob the way back in by giving him the dream of the ladder set up on the earth, with the top of it reaching to heaven (Gen. 28:12). The angels of God were ascending and descending on it.

In fact, that ladder was symbolic of Christ. Concerning this very thing, Jesus said of Himself, even as He began His public ministry, *"Verily, verily, I say unto you, Hereafter you shall see heaven open, and the angels of God ascending and descending upon the Son of Man"* (Jn. 1:51).

THE FALL

When Adam and Eve were driven out of the garden, they went into a world that everywhere exhibited the lamentable results of the fall. The cherubim with the flaming sword did forbid fallen man to pluck the fruit of the Tree of Life, but God's revelation would point him to the death and resurrection of the seed of the woman wherein life would be found beyond the pallor of death, and so it was!

As a consequence, Adam was a safer man outside the bounds of Paradise than he would have been within in his fallen state, and for this reason: within, his life depended upon himself, whereas outside, it depended upon another, even a promised Christ.

If the cherubim and flaming sword closed up the way to Paradise, which they were forced to do, the Lord Jesus Christ has opened a new and living way into the holiest of all. *"I am the way, the truth, and the life: no man comes unto the Father, but by Me"* (Jn. 14:6; Heb. 10:20).

In the knowledge of all of this, the believer now moves onward through a world that is under the curse—where the traces of sin are visible on all hands. Mackintosh said, "He has found his way, by faith, and we speak of faith in Christ and Him crucified, to the bosom of the Father; and while he can secretly repose there, he is cheered by the blessed assurance that the One who has conducted him thither is gone to prepare a place in the many mansions of the Father's house, and that He will soon come again and receive him unto Himself, amid the glory of the Father's kingdom."[15]

Join all the glorious names
Of wisdom, love, and power,
That ever mortals knew,
That angels ever bore:
All are too poor to speak His worth,
Too poor to set my Saviour forth.

Great Prophet of my God,
My tongue would bless Your name:
By Thee the joyful news
Of our salvation came,
The joyful news of sins forgiven,
Of hell subdued and peace with heaven.

Jesus, my great High Priest,
Offered His blood, and died;
My guilty conscience seeks
No sacrifice beside:
His powerful blood did once atone,
And now it pleads before the throne.

You are my counselor,
My pattern, and my guide,
And You my shepherd are;
Oh, keep me near Your side;
Nor let my feet e're turn astray,
To wander in the crooked way.

My Saviour and my Lord,
My Conqueror and my King,
Your scepter and Your sword,
Your reigning grace I sing:
Thine is the power, behold I sit
In willing bonds beneath Your feet.

REFERENCES

INTRODUCTION

[1] Joseph S. Exell, *Biblical Illustrator, Volume 1,* (Delmarva Publications, Inc., 2015).

CHAPTER 1

[1] George Williams, *William's Complete Bible Commentary,* (Grand Rapids, Kregel Publications, 1994) p. 9.

[2] Matthew Henry & Thomas Scott, *A Commentary on the Holy Bible: Genesis to Deuteronomy,* (The Religious Tract Society), p. 17.

[3] H. D. M. Spence, *The Pulpit Commentary: Genesis 1:11,* (Grand Rapids, Eerdmans Publishing Company, 1978).

[4] H. D. M. Spence, *The Pulpit Commentary: Genesis 1:21,* (Grand Rapids, Eerdmans Publishing Company, 1978).

[5] Matthew Henry & Thomas Scott, *A Commentary on the Holy Bible: Genesis to Deuteronomy,* The Religious Tract Society.

[6] H. D. M. Spence, *The Pulpit Commentary: Genesis,* (Grand Rapids, Eerdmans Publishing Company, 1978).

[7] Matthew Henry & Thomas Scott, *A Commentary on the Holy Bible: Genesis to Deuteronomy,* (The Religious Tract Society), p. 5.

CHAPTER 2

[1] George Williams, *William's Complete Bible Commentary,* (Grand Rapids, Kregel Publications, 1994), p. 9.

[2] George Williams, *William's Complete Bible Commentary,* (Grand Rapids, Kregel Publications, 1994), p. 10.

[3] Franz Delitzsch, *Commentary on the Old Testament,* (Titus Books, 2014).

[4] *Ellicott's Commentary on the Whole Bible,* (Zondervan Publishing House, New York, 1880).

[5] C. H. Mackintosh, *Notes on the Book of Genesis,* (New York, Loizeaux Brothers, 1880).

[6] C. H. Mackintosh, *Notes on the Pentateuch: The Book of Genesis,* (New York, Loizeaux Brothers, 1880).

7 *Ellicott's Commentary on the Whole Bible*, (Zondervan Publishing House, New York, 1880), p. 22.

8 Stanley M. Horton, *Genesis: The Promise of Blessing*, (World Library Press, Missouri, 1996).

CHAPTER 3

1 *The Preacher's Complete Homiletical Commentary on the Old Testament: Genesis*, (Funk & Wagnalls, 1892), p. 63.

2 Matthew Henry, *Exposition of the Old and New Testament: Volume I*, (University of Lausanne, 1828), p. 16.

3 *Ibid.*

4 George Williams, *William's Complete Bible Commentary*, (Grand Rapids, Kregel Publications, 1994), p. 10.

5 H. D. M. Spence, *The Pulpit Commentary: Genesis 3:9-10*, (Grand Rapids, Eerdmans Publishing Company, 1978), p. 64.

6 *Ibid.*

7 Matthew Henry, *Exposition of the Old and New Testament: Volume I*, (University of Lausanne, 1828), p. 19.

8 *Ibid.*

[9] *Ellicott's Commentary on the Whole Bible,* (Zondervan Publishing House, New York, 1880).

[10] Matthew Henry, *Exposition of the Old and New Testament: Volume I,* (University of Lausanne, 1828), p. 16.

[11] *Ellicott's Commentary on the Whole Bible,* (Zondervan Publishing House, New York, 1880).

[12] Matthew Henry, *Exposition of the Old and New Testament: Volume I,* (University of Lausanne, 1828), p. 17.

[13] H. D. M. Spence, *The Pulpit Commentary: Genesis,* (Grand Rapids, Eerdmans Publishing Company, 1978), p. 74.

[14] *Ibid.*

[15] C. H. Mackintosh, *Notes on the Book of Genesis,* (New York, Loizeaux Brothers, 1880).

ABOUT EVANGELIST JIMMY SWAGGART

The Rev. Jimmy Swaggart is a Pentecostal evangelist whose anointed preaching and teaching has drawn multitudes to the Cross of Christ since 1955.

As an author, he has written more than 50 books, commentaries, study guides, and The Expositor's Study Bible, which has sold more than 2.5 million copies.

As an award-winning musician and singer, Brother Swaggart has recorded more than 50 gospel albums and sold nearly 16 million recordings worldwide.

For more than six decades, Brother Swaggart has channeled his preaching and music ministry through multiple media venues including print, radio, television and the Internet.

In 2010, Jimmy Swaggart Ministries launched its own cable channel, SonLife Broadcasting Network, which airs 24 hours a day to a potential viewing audience of more than 1 billion people around the globe.

Brother Swaggart also pastors Family Worship Center in Baton Rouge, Louisiana, the church home and headquarters of Jimmy Swaggart Ministries.

Jimmy Swaggart Ministries materials can be found at **www.jsm.org**.